THE MORAL CASE FOR CONSERVATISM

THE MORAL CASE
FOR CONSERVATISM

SAMUEL BURGESS

Wilberforce Publications
London

First published in Great Britain in 2019 by
Wilberforce Publications Limited
70 Wimpole Street, London W1G 8AX

Wilberforce Publications Limited is a wholly owned subsidiary of Christian Concern

ISBN 978-1-9995842-3-8

Printed in Great Britain by Imprint Digital, Exeter

Contents

INTRODUCTION

On the evening of the 25th October 1917, Vladimir Lenin stood in the cold autumn air, his heart racing, as Bolshevik forces streamed into Petrograd and seized control of key government buildings. As the day drew on, the magnificent Winter Palace that had housed the Tsars for two centuries was overrun. A new era had dawned on Russia, an era that would liberate the long oppressed working classes and bring enlightenment, first to Russia and then to mankind.

But the great plan failed. Communism did not turn out to be the saviour of the proletariat as its prophets predicted. Within two years the Bolsheviks were ruthlessly purging those who disagreed with them. Within a decade they ruled by dictatorship with an iron fist. Over the course of the twentieth century over 100 million deaths ensued at the hands of communist governments and humanity learned a harrowing lesson in the frailty of human nature and the danger of utopian visions.

I start this book with the story of communism because it teaches us a lesson of singular importance: human progress is not inevitable. It is true that human civilisation has taken great leaps forward, technologically and ethically. We have travelled along a tortuous path, from the primitive hunting bands of our Palaeolithic forefathers. This juddering journey has continued to the present day, but it has been filled with lengthy detours and empty cul-de-sacs, some of which have required costly u-turns. Along the route, we have witnessed the tyranny of absolute kingship, the evils of communism, the purges of revolutionary liberalism and the horrors of fascism.

As 21st Century British citizens it is easy to assume that a stable social order in which we are free to enjoy social pleasures, pursue intellectual interests and associate with whom we choose, is the historical norm. The reality is that we find ourselves in a uniquely privileged position in human history within a social order that has been purchased at inestimable cost. This book is motivated by the conviction that if we become careless and underestimate how unique that social order is, then we will lose it.

Conservatism is not concerned with preventing change, but it is concerned with ensuring that the changes made within a nation are necessary and beneficial. In this book, each chapter will deal with a different area of our public life challenged in the modern world. In each of these areas I will explain why conservatism offers answers of enduring relevance.

The necessity for an intellectual defence of conservatism arises as the spectre of hard left socialism and radical liberalism present themselves as a growing presence in our society. Worryingly, these trends are particularly resurgent among the nation's youth. The General Election of 2017 should cause grave concern for conservatives. Two in three first-time voters chose to support a hard left socialist candidate, while fewer than one in five young voters supported the Conservative Party. It is only over the age of 47 that a voter is now more likely to vote Conservative than Labour.[1]

Even more troublingly, elements of the Conservative Party have shown signs that they have forgotten the very meaning of conservatism. The major parties in British politics today often employ a political discourse which, in terms of its vocabulary and basic ideas, is far more redolent of the liberal tradition than it is of British conservatism.

This has not gone undetected by grass roots conservatives. In response to the widespread liberalisation of political parties, there has been a backlash across Europe and North America in favour of parties that represent patriotism over cosmopolitanism, the working man over the political technocrat and a reassertion of pride in local culture and national history.

In this book, we will look at why these instincts are healthy and a fundamental part of a functioning society, but we will also look at how conservatism helps to limit these deeply human instincts and prevent them from degenerating into blind nationalism. We will see where the central convictions of the tradition emerge from and the logic behind them. But most importantly we will see that there is above all a moral case to be made for conservatism, as a body of principles which preserve freedom and human dignity in the face of their detractors. If communist rule in the twentieth century taught us anything, it is that political ideas matter and the stakes could not be any higher.

Chapter One

A BRIEF HISTORY OF CONSERVATISM

It is important to clarify from the outset what is meant by conservatism, since by meaning too much the term can end up meaning very little. A variety of political creeds across the world today call themselves 'conservative'. As with all political labels we must be careful not to assume that a commonality of name implies a commonality of belief. There are, for example, American political organisations which identify as 'conservative' which would to a British mind be considered libertarian. Moreover, conservative groups have been engaged in diverse debates in different contexts and this has led to various articulations of the conservative philosophy. The US Southern Agrarians of the 1930s, for example, held a different set of concerns to the French conservatives of the 1870s.

There is no binding creed which unites the body of sentiments known as conservatism, precisely because its principles commend themselves in a different manner within different contexts. This is why conservatives from Edmund Burke to Russell Kirk have spoken of a disposition towards enduring truths as opposed to a rigid ideology. Nevertheless, there is a clear historical lineage of Anglophone conservative thinkers who articulate a set of political principles established upon similar philosophical foundations. It is this tradition that we shall explore. A comprehensive, though not exhaustive, list of these principles might be helpful from the outset.

I take them to be:

Moral and philosophical realism
An accurate account of human nature
A scepticism about abstract ideologies
A belief in freedom under law
The preservation of healthy customs and institutions
Limited government and the primacy of civil society

Conservatism therefore does not simply advocate a procedural conservation of the status quo; it consists in a number of substantive beliefs. Nevertheless, it derives its name from the fifth principle I have enumerated: the preservation of healthy customs and institutions.

Human societies are not like laboratory experiments, there is not a control group we can run our political systems against and analyse how well they have performed. Our failed experiments have resulted in atrocities, civil wars and famines. In response to each failure our social attitudes have changed, our systems of government have bulwarked themselves against a repetition of such calamities, our legislation and corpus of law has adapted to prevent any repetition of past failures. These adaptations do not just occur in response to the calamities of the past, but to the minute daily violations of justice that take place in the routine of everyday life. It is these 'adaptations' against injustice, inhumanity and lawlessness which conservatism hopes to preserve in the social body.

Critically, there must be a feedback loop which forces a society to change and adapt. In nature, the gradual change of an organism is driven by the external stimuli of competition in its natural environment. This external competitive pressure does exist for human societies, but the most cogent force of change is the internal stimulus of political demand. This of course is the basis for democracy: the belief that a society will, under the weight of internal political pressure, mould itself into an arrangement that is beneficial for all of its members. One famous landmark of democratisation in Britain is the Magna Carta, but the Provisions of Oxford, the Petition of Right, the Glorious Revolution, the 1832 Reform Act, as well as the 1918 and 1969 Representation of the People Acts, are all significant landmarks upon our national journey to opening this feedback loop, so that the executive government is obliged

10

to comply with the demands of the people.

Democracies are founded on the conviction that societies should not be dictated to by the brave or the brilliant, but rather by the common consent of the many. Winston Churchill is said to have joked that 'the best argument against democracy is a five minute conversation with the average voter'. Yet the beauty of democracy is that it does not require any single person to understand the complexities of a political question. It is the ability of each individual to articulate how government policies are touching them in their lives, from their uniquely situated point of view, that makes the 'hive' mind of democracy a far more intelligent governor than any ruler or official. As Edmund Burke put it, 'the individual is foolish, the species is wise'.

Conservatism is innately democratic, as it relies on organic change as opposed to autocratic stipulation. This preservation of tried patterns has led us to a system of government and a social order that works for us as a people, with our peculiar habits, climate, temper and geography. Conservatism is never static, as we are always adapting and changing, but changes occur in small gradations, as we retain the vast evolved body that has been bequeathed to us by the errors and innovations of the past.

Yet, as we have seen, this conviction is not all that conservatism consists of. To profess social conservation alone would be to present the bones of conservatism and forego its soul. Conservatism has never been solely a dry political philosophy, but rather, since Burke's first articulation of its principles, it has been rooted in the belief that the political is inseparable from the social, the moral and indeed the religious. They are bound together in a holistic vision of the universe that perceives human flourishing to be more than just a political endeavour. The conservative tradition has remained unapologetic for this fact, in the conviction that the great metaphysical truths inevitably determine political truths.

In 1926 Stanley Baldwin wrote:

Disraeli laid our principles down at the Crystal Palace many years ago, and you cannot go wrong if you stick to them. There were: 'the maintenance of our institutions and of our religion; the preservation of our Empire, and the improvement in the condition of our people'.

If there is one thing which Disraeli stressed... it was the maintenance of religion.

Conservation then is not simply commended for conservation's sake, but it is a product of a much broader moral vision. These are themes we will return to throughout this book.

The basic ideas which lie at the heart of conservatism go back much further than any self-conscious articulation of a British political tradition. The roots of the conservative tradition are found in the fertile soil of the English common law. The English tradition of common law, which was formalised in the twelfth century had, from the outset, a belief in the primacy of the rule of law which bound the rulers as well as the ruled, the value of precedent, and the accountability of political rule to God's moral law, which became the bedrock of modern conservatism.

Drawing heavily upon the common law tradition, the earliest recognisable political work with conservative themes came from a theological perspective, in the thought of Richard Hooker (b. 1554). Hooker's most notable work was *On the Laws of Ecclesiastical Polity*. In this work he defended England's established institutions (ecclesiastical, legal and political) and rebutted those puritans who sought to recast them on the basis of scripture detached from all tradition (*sola scriptura*). His key argument, echoed by Burke, was that such individuals were not exhibiting any humility in their desire to dispose of time honoured institutions, and they were therefore guilty of pride. In his work he emphasised the joint operation of reason, law and tradition. He made the case that laws and institutions should be diverse and suited to the temper of a particular people, as long as they did not contravene the moral law. His arguments would become recurrent themes of the conservative tradition.

The father of conservatism is generally accepted to be the Whig statesman Edmund Burke (b. 1729). Burke was a behemoth of British politics, whose career bestrode the eighteenth century. He is famous for denouncing the French Revolution at a time when many liberals supported it and for being a great social reformer at home. Like Hooker, his political ideas are undergirded by a strong belief in a divinely created moral order. Burke's most famous work was his *Reflections on the Revolution in France*, in which he expressed his horror at the manner in which the French had torn down their ancient state in the hope of rebuilding it on the basis of pure reason. Burke's pessimism at this endeavour was to be vindicated, as the French political project degenerated into violence, anarchy and terror.

Following the radicalism of the eighteenth century, the early nineteenth century saw the first articulations of self-consciously conservative political thought. Edmund Burke exercised an enormous influence over the subsequent generations at Westminster, including men such as William Pitt the Younger, who had to deal with the turbulent aftermath of the French Revolution. Following Pitt's death in 1806 a faction of his acolytes emerged, who sought to continue his principles of government. In 1830 the *Quarterly Review* suggested the term 'Conservative Party' for this faction. It was a name adopted by Robert Peel, when he became Prime Minister in 1834 and the British Conservative Party was born. It remains the oldest political party in the world.

The Conservative Party retained widespread support throughout the nineteenth century, enjoying ten separate administrations in office. During this period Burke's intellectual legacy was continued by George Canning, The Duke of Wellington, Robert Peel, The Marquess of Salisbury and, perhaps most famous of all, Benjamin Disraeli. Each of these figures responded to the exigencies of their own era with a recognisably conservative philosophy. Burke's scepticism towards grand ideologies was one reason that Britain, almost alone in Europe, survived the nineteenth century without enduring revolutions which beset many of the great European monarchies in 1848. Once again, Britain's conservative instincts were sound, as the revolutions which swept across Europe proved to bring even greater repression in many countries, particularly Prussia and the lands of the Habsburg Empire. Britain followed Edmund Burke's caution that the worst way to reform a state was by its subversion; instead, Burke commended treating 'the faults of the state as to the wounds of a father'.[2]

In the twentieth century conservatism as a political force continued to dominate British politics. Stanley Baldwin, Winston Churchill, Anthony Eden and Harold Macmillan are just some of the Conservative prime ministers that remain significant figures in British history.

There is one Prime Minister who defined the popular characterisation of modern British conservatism more than any other: Margaret Thatcher. Under the influence of libertarian thinkers, such as Friedrich Hayek, Thatcher sought to promote a property owning democracy and break the power that the trade unions had over Britain. Thatcher's administrations did not, however, represent a complete break with the 'One Nation' Conservatism of Disraeli. She recognised the limited role of government and the truth that if the government was going to provide public services, then the private sector must be strong enough to fund this enterprise.

Her central conviction was that the great engines of private industry would only serve the people if they were profitable enough to return money to the public purse. Whether her rapid denationalisation of British owned industry was handled correctly is a question we shall return to in this book. Regrettably, and perhaps unfairly, Thatcher's legacy has resulted in a popular association between conservatism and a radically free market approach to economics, which privileges the rich to the detriment of working class communities. A poll conducted by Lord Ashcroft in 2013 showed that sixty-four per cent of the British electorate believed the Conservative Party to be the party of the rich. The fallout of this consensus has been a historical amnesia about the role conservatism has played in pioneering social reform.

One of the great modern myths is that conservatism as a philosophy has always been concerned with preserving the interests of a small self-serving clique at the expense of the rest of the population. A casual glance at the history of the Conservative Party demonstrates that this could not be further from the truth. The conservative philosophy has been a great engine of social reform for at least two hundred years in Great Britain.

In 1802, Robert Peel's Health and Morals of Apprentices Act, limited the hours of factory workers, gave them a basic education and improved their working conditions.[3] The limited success of this Act was followed by his more effective 1819 Cotton Mills and Factories Act. William Wilberforce's lifelong endeavour to abolish the slave trade famously came to fruition in 1807. While he was an independent member of parliament, his Christian faith instilled in him a profound social conservatism, matched only by his humanitarian impulse.

In 1875 Benjamin Disraeli, a man possessed of a piquant wit and a passion for the poor, passed the Public Health Act, which helped to clear slums, introduce drainage, pave streets and improve sanitation. Similarly, Lord Salisbury pioneered the Housing of the Working Classes Bill in 1885, forcing landlords to improve squalid living conditions. In 1902 the Conservative Party, under Arthur Balfour, increased the standard of education across the country and in 1928 Stanley Baldwin's conservative government passed the Representation of the People Act bringing equal franchise to men and women. Following the Second World War, Harold Macmillan passed the 1957 Housing Act to ensure that housing was fit for human habitation, following this up with the 1961 Factories Act to protect factory workers. This tradition of Conservative party social reform has continued into the twentieth century under David Cameron, who adopted a number of policies to increase the wealth and social mobility for the poorest in society, including a substantial rise in the income tax threshold.

In the chapters ahead, we will scrutinise some of the myths that have come to surround conservatism. We will look in some detail at the huge social progress that conservatives have achieved and how the moral heart of their tradition compelled them to improve society for the most vulnerable.

Intellectual tributaries

British conservatism is not built upon the political party alone. Britain also has deep intellectual reservoirs that have sustained and revitalised the tradition in each succeeding generation as their tributaries have flowed into popular public discourse. Some of these thinkers have been religious figures, some poets, some writers.

In 1830 Samuel Taylor Coleridge, once a radical and a supporter of the French Revolution, published *On the Constitution of the Church and State*. In it, he argued against the rationalism of his day, that our ancient political arrangements are 'founded either in the nature of things or in the necessities of our nature', as well as making the case for widespread education, biblical teaching and the relief of poverty. Wordsworth too, embarked on a personal journey from radicalism to social conservatism, while John Ruskin's criticism of art and architecture was steeped in the conviction that the local, the traditional and the beautiful must be recovered.

John Henry Newman and John Keble did in the ecclesiastical realm what others did in the political, arguing for the recovery of tradition and cautioning against moral deprivation. They both emphasised the spiritual and organic qualities of society, in the face of rapid industrialisation. They opposed the idea that material acquisition alone would satisfy the spiritual core of man's nature.

In the twentieth century T. S. Eliot was the most influential proponent of conservatism. His thought emerged amidst a new and seemingly meaningless modernity, which had detached itself from traditional mores and meaning. G. K. Chesterton, Christopher Dawson and C. S. Lewis are just some of the other names which are associated with social conservatism, vitalising the tradition through essays, historical study and narrative fiction.

The Character of a Nation

It has often been suggested that there is a natural conservatism about the British people who, since the eighteenth century, have been known by their continental contemporaries as traditionalists, satirists and lovers of free speech. In the middle of the eighteenth century, French philosophes, such as Voltaire, who visited England, were astonished by the liberties the British enjoyed. Voltaire wrote in a letter to his friend Thierot: 'I will acquaint you with the character of this strange people, an unaccountable nation fond of their liberty'. He persistently referred to the liberties of the British, contrasting this with French autocracy.

This historical attachment to liberty is illustrated by the Magna Carta. Rudyard Kipling's poem *The Reeds of Runnymede* captures the intractable English nature:

> At Runnymede, at Runnymede,
> Oh, hear the reeds at Runnymede;
> "You mustn't sell, delay, deny,
> A freeman's right or liberty.
> It makes the stubborn Englishry,
> We saw 'em roused at Runnymede!

16

And still when Mob or Monarch lays
Too rude a hand on English ways,
The whisper wakes, the shudder plays,
Across the reeds at Runnymede.

In *King John*, Shakespeare wrote, 'This England never did, nor never shall, Lie at the proud foot of a conqueror'. While William Wordsworth believed 'We must be free or die who speak the tongue, That Shakespeare spake, the faith and morals hold Which Milton held.'

This attachment to liberty has gone hand in hand with a proclivity towards commerce and civil associations of all kinds; Napoleon scornfully caricatured England as 'a nation of shopkeepers'. The offspring of commerce is of course property. The keen attachment of individuals to their small stake in society is one of the things which has historically guarded Britain from the predations of the socialist state. As James Otis wrote, 'One of the most essential branches of English liberty is the freedom of one's house.' Even as early as 1644, English judge Sir Edward Coke was quoted as saying 'For a man's house is his castle.'

While liberty, commerce and property are key features identified with Britishness, they are all rooted in a fourth and more ancient English idea. That idea is law. The quiet but insistent British attachment to liberty was not the radical revolutionary freedom professed by the libertines of the continent. Quite to the contrary, the British attachment to liberty, exemplified by Magna Carta, has been premised on the idea that personal freedom is secured by the nation's laws and traditions. This idea is central to conservatism.

In the following chapters we will explore this web of ideas. As we work through eight key areas of our shared public life, I will show how the principles I have enumerated logically interlock as a body of political thought, but more significantly how, by accident or design, they attain moral ends which serve the common good. Sometimes the argument may extend beyond the narrow confines of politics *per se*. These excursions are embarked upon in the conviction that if we want to answer the big political questions, then we must delve into even more fundamental issues. The first idea we will look at is 'The Nation State'.

Chapter Two

THE NATION STATE

I vow to thee, my country, all earthly things above,
Entire and whole and perfect, the service of my love
– Sir Cecil Spring Rice

National Community

An alien who landed in Russia during the summer of 2018 would likely
be bemused by the spectacle of the World Cup. It would witness grown
men weeping in their seats, grandmothers jumping in unrestrained
euphoria, children peeking breathlessly through their fingers, their
emotions rising and falling as quickly as the small leather ball upon
which they are transfixed. It is of course not simply the game itself which
fixates whole nations upon a hundred yards of hallowed turf. It is the
sense that eleven players are a representation of ourselves, that they are
an exhibition of the best we as a community have to offer. With them
the nation stands or falls, like a modern day gladiatorial contest. So why
is it that we are so emotionally invested in our nations?

What appears to us today as the most natural unit of governance was,
until the fourteenth century, largely unknown in Europe. Before this time
European people mostly defined themselves in relation to the feudal
estate or principality in which they lived. A peasant would consider
herself a resident of Normandy or Aquitaine, not France. But over the
next two hundred years an astonishing transition of identity took place.
It was not that local identities disappeared – a resident of Normandy
still continued to identify with Normandy – but the primacy of local
loyalties was usurped by larger communal identities which captured the
hearts and minds of Europeans for the first time. The nation state had
been born. England, France, Spain and Russia would emerge as the first
examples of this new form of communal order.

A number of events expedited this transition, but there were two of supreme importance: firstly, the reformation, which substituted the ambiguous fealty of rulers to the papacy for the unequivocal political rule of national sovereigns. This transition was finalised following the seventeenth century wars of religion in the Peace of Westphalia (1648), which resolved that the ruler of a region would decide its religion, an idea first articulated in the Peace of Augsburg by the phrase *cuius regio, eius religio* ('whose realm, his religion'). The second event was the industrial revolution which, through economic wealth and improved infrastructure, fostered a clear national consciousness in rapidly industrialising nations.

By the late nineteenth century the major powers of Europe were nations that had transitioned from agrarian to industrial societies. For some nations this involved the unification of principalities and provinces for the first time; the most notable cases being Belgium which formed in 1831, with Italy and Germany each unifying in 1871. In undergoing this transition nations broke down the regional differences within their borders, standardised their laws and languages and centralised their currencies and military forces.

With the perspective of modern historical research, we can look over our shoulder and survey the vast catalogue of communal identities that our species has adopted: from the tribe to the ethnic group, the religious sect to the empire, the feudal serfdom to the principality, the duchy to the nation state. However, in maintaining peace, developing civilisation, and enriching the material wealth of its inhabitants, the nation state is without equal. It has been by far the most successful social project our species has innovated. As the MEP Daniel Hannan put it, 'it is extremely rare to find justice, freedom, or representative government flourishing in any context other than a nation-state.'[4] The key reason for this fact is that it is a form of society which allows us to associate with each other on a grand scale, while still holding fundamental values in common.

A nation consists in the unified corporate agency of professional institutions, government bodies, civil associations and most fundamentally, local communities. Importantly, these disparate institutions are held in communion by a broad consensus of moral values. The common agency of a nation is predicated upon a shared locality – a state. The nation state presupposes a shared good and a mutual enrichment between a people. Contrary to social contract theorists such as Thomas Hobbes, nations are not forged only through expedient impulses, such as a desire for protection, but by constructive patterns of behaviour which breed trust, familiarity and friendship.

The small platoons of the nation state

Over the past two decades there has been a resurgence of interest in civil society. Western governments and policy units seem to have come to the conclusion that communities really are central to human wellbeing.[5]

The etymology of the word 'community' is latinate, deriving from *communitatem* which meant to hold something in common ownership. This phrase gives us an insight into what a national community is. It is not one large tribe, but rather hundreds of small tribes bound together by cultural commonalities.

In Edmund Burke's *Reflections on the Revolution in France* he wrote:

> We begin our public affections in our families. We pass on to our neighbourhoods, and our habitual provincial connexions... The love to the whole is not extinguished by this subordinate partiality.. it is a sort of elemental training to those higher and more large regards, by which alone men come to be affected, as with their own concern, in the prosperity of a kingdom.

Burke's argument is that our love for those things which we hold in common with others in our local communities does not make us inward looking and parochial, but conversely it teaches us *how* to love a community, *how* to serve a society and, ultimately, it guides our affections towards larger horizons.[6] Burke recognises that nation states have succeeded in taking the innate human desire for a small tribe and connecting this parochial attachment to a far greater body, by associating the nation with the values, symbols and ideas with which we have become familiarised in our local context.

We might imagine a child raised in Istanbul who inevitably becomes attuned to the daily rhythm of life on the banks of the Bosphorus. The morning call to prayer as she wakes, the rich smell of roast chestnuts and spices on her way to school, the bustle of the Grand Bazaar in the early evening, the sun setting behind the familiar minarets of the Hagia Sophia. As she develops a love for such small things, they act as an icon, leading her affections to something greater than herself. She comes to care about her surroundings, her local community and her countrymen. When she says she loves Turkey, she cannot possibly be claiming to know and love Konya, Kas, Antalya and Marmaris, which she has never visited. Rather, she feels Istanbul to be a microcosm of the whole.

She can identify that there are elements of her life in Istanbul which are shared in common by all Turks as an expression of their shared values and history. As she walks the old city walls she is reminded of the common story of her people and the exploits of her ancestors. She senses that somehow their feats are still threaded into the fabric of her society. As she grows she comes to notice the subtle signposts of history pointing backwards to bygone cultures and conquests, which have ebbed and flowed through the centuries. These whispered vestiges of the past draw her into a greater story, one filled with duty, sacrifice and corporate endeavour. It is a narrative which has birthed the nation she knows today. Her affection for Turkey is rooted in her love for the familiar characteristics of the corporate body.

As Edmund Burke pointed out, it is in our local associations that we 'are given many little images of the great country in which the heart [finds] something it [can] fill'. Our actions align themselves with our affections. In this way we are drawn into the common life of a community. At the most basic level we might think of the parents who nurture their children, the boy who supports his football team, the community activist who picks litter in the local park. The structures of civil society facilitate altruism, in which we are motivated to do that which simultaneously serves our own interest and the interests of the community. As naturally social beings, it should be no surprise to us that our personal joy is often realised in the context of enriching the corporate body of which we are a part.

What follows from this is that, if a nation is to cohere, then though communities may be divergent in some areas, they must have deep currents of underlying commonality. When the average Athenian ceases to feel a sense of commonality and shared interest with a Thessalonian, then the idea of 'Greece' will be in perilous straits.

This sense of shared kinship is the soil of democracy. It is only when we feel a tacit connection with our countrymen that we have the empathy for democracy to flourish. This connection need not be wholly altruistic, nor is it entirely self-serving. The bonds of nationhood simply require the acknowledgement that, in some sense, our destinies are shared; our common care for each other and for our nation will be mutually enriching.

Following the Second World War there was a popular hope for a world government that would preclude the possibility of nuclear weapons ever being used between nations again. This hope was articulated by the most eminent British philosopher of the twentieth century, the Fabian socialist Bertrand Russell. Russell argued that 'unification under a single government is probably necessary unless we are to acquiesce in either a return to barbarism or the extinction of the human race'. Russell did concede that there would likely be 'a psychological difficulty about a single world government.' In his view 'the chief source of social cohesion in the past... has been war: the passions that inspire a feeling of unity are hate and fear.'[7]

It is easy to see how Russell came to these conclusions in the immediate aftermath of the social unity that the war had inspired in Britain.[8] Yet, his conclusion seems entirely backward. In the mundane course of everyday life, it is not the imminent fear of war and the hatred of others that inspires national affection but, rather, it is our love that draws us towards its object. When crowds turn out to see a royal wedding or to celebrate their independence day, they are united in a shared love for their country and what it represents. In times of external threat this love can indeed impel us to unite in a shared antipathy towards an aggressor but, for most, these feelings are transient and unsustainable over a lifetime. It is not because of conflict that we form community, but more often, it is because of our love for our community that we are occasionally drawn into conflict.

Unlike the nation state, the sort of transnational government that Russell alluded to seems the most likely form of social organisation to inspire conflict, precisely because it is so large a monolith that, by endeavouring to mean all things to all people, it means nothing and therefore has no purchase upon people's hearts. The result is a paralysing deficit of the civic consciousness which is necessary for democracy and the self identification of a people with their government. The end result of such transnational governance is invariably clusters of organic human communities being coerced into an unwilling coherence and compliance with the dictats of an alien state.

Peace under such circumstances would necessarily be imposed by authoritarian rule. The preservation of human freedom must be predicated on free choice, which leaves open the possibility of conflict.[9] But the relationships between nation states represent the best way to regulate those disagreements while preserving the self-determination of nations. Differences of interest can and do arise between them but these are mitigated by international agreements which seek to deter and mediate conflict. Such an international order of nation states encourages the respectful acceptance of difference within clearly defined moral limits. To misquote Winston Churchill, this is the worst form of international order, apart from all the others that have been tried.

In democratic terms, transnational governments inevitably leave individuals feeling deeply frustrated at their inability to effect change to their way of life while being governed by people with whom they perceive no commonality; this was *in extremis* the grievance against empire. The more proximate the form of government to the common person, the more empowered citizens will feel, the more satiated their desire to effect change will be, and the more engaged they will become in their society.[10]

It is not a coincidence that the evolution of democracy was coterminous with that of the nation state. Nations emerge where settled patterns of human behaviour germinate commonalities in a people. By the time Otto von Bismarck unified the German states in the late nineteenth century, its shared language, infrastructure and customs meant that the unification process was possible, but even then the process was not purely administrative. Bismarck placed a strong emphasis on the Germanisation of the people, promoting a common history and waging a *Kulturkampf* against the influence of the Catholic Church. Even during the First World War Bavarians and Prussians did not think of themselves as an entirely unified people. If a nation is to succeed, this process of common identification must occur naturally. We might think of contiguous townships that over time grow conurbations, which eventually meet and interact, until they are one organic entity. Nations are gestated and born; if they are mandated they are likely, sooner or later, to founder.

It is for these reasons that modern efforts to instate transnational modes of government have failed. The European Union, like the Soviet Union before it, perceives itself as a progressive development towards a new form of community in which the primacy of national identity is transplanted by a new transnational consciousness. In truth, the number of British people who genuinely have transnational identities is a stunningly small percentage of the population (only 2.6 per cent of the population identify as being European over being British.)[11] This is unsurprising, when we reflect on the fact that nations settle their identity as they settle their borders, over the course of generations through external conflict, internal wrestling and the harmonising influence of common custom. In Burke's phrase, regions are 'formed by habit and not by a sudden jerk of authority'.[12]

To see what happens when nations as culturally disparate as Greece and Germany have a supranational identity superimposed upon them, we need look no further than the events of 2012.

National vs Transnational governments

In February 2012 the world was confronted with the spectacle of around 80,000 Greeks protesting in Athens against punitive, German backed, austerity measures. The Greek government was effectively held to ransom by the European Troika (the EC, the ECB and the IMF) who insisted on budget cuts and austerity in return for further loans to prevent a default on their debt.[13] The feeling of oppression emerged from the fact the Greek government was unable to pay their existing debts, due in part to the lack of fiscal sovereignty entailed in the European single currency. The only option was to pursue an unwanted course of fiscal austerity. The protests soon turned to rioting. There were reportedly 40 buildings set on fire, followed by widespread damage and attacks on dozens of police officers.[14]

By autumn, when Chancellor Merkel visited Athens, the Greek people seemed united in anger at their treatment by supranational powers. One of the most striking sights was the burning in effigy of the German Chancellor; some Greeks even flew swastikas, resurrecting the bitter memories of the Nazi subjugation of Greece. These two culturally and economically disparate countries unsurprisingly found themselves at loggerheads. Germans were accusing Greeks of indolence; Greeks were accusing Germans of exploitation. Inevitably, as the German people felt the Greeks threatened their own economic fortunes, they began to become more muscular in their treatment of Greece. Germany's finance minister, Wolfgang Schäuble, even suggested the imposition of a Sparkommissar to control Greek finances. The resentment of the Greek people has smouldered on long after the immediate crisis subsided.

What the European Union failed to recognise is that the Greeks have a different temperament, different language, different economy and a different history to the Germans. The Greeks did not feel themselves to be the same people as the Germans; quite to the contrary, they felt that a foreign people were foisting unwanted economic measures on them to serve their own purposes. This is the same suspicion that has troubled the British in their criticism of France's capitalisation upon the Common Agricultural Policy.[15] When people primarily identify as national, not transnational, citizens then they will inevitably use a transnational body to manoeuvre for their own ends at the expense of others. Is it any surprise that there is such a disparity of opinion between the nations of Europe as to the correct course of action in a time of crisis? Despite seeing itself as the great guarantor of peace in Europe, the European Union's culturally monotone approach to politics has repeatedly caused consternation amongst its member states.

In 2018 Angela Merkel and Emmanuel Macron both called for the creation of a European army. The creation of such an army would mean that if there was civil unrest in Italy (let us say in protest to an EU Directive), then soldiers from Germany or France could feasibly be called in to suppress the disorder. Italians may well permit law enforcement by their own countrymen who they feel a commonality with, but would they really allow German or French soldiers to perform this role? Yet they could be left without grounds for remonstration against such an occupation by European troops, because they are ostensibly European citizens under a European parliament. Such a hypothetical circumstance illustrates the dangers lurking behind the idea of a federal European identity in which people do not primarily identify as Europeans.

Despite the issues which beset transnational institutions, there remains a prevailing belief among elements of our society that the nation state is something of a barbaric cultural artefact which more enlightened members of society have already outgrown. In 1993 the French diplomat Jean-Marie Guéhenno published a book called 'The End of the Nation State', in which he made the case that the nation state would soon become obsolete. This is a view that was reiterated at the LSE in 2018 by the European Parliament's representative in the Brexit negotiations, Guy Verhofstadt. Interestingly, one of Guéhenno's key examples of a federation which has outflanked the fusty old nation state is the European Union. Yet even a federal Europe, in his view, would 'no longer correspond to the realities of a networked age, liberated from the constraints, and advantages, of geography'.[16] Similarly, the Czech political theorist Alex Tomsky said on the BBC: 'The nation state is a very obsolete idea of course. It's an idea of the 19th century as we all know. I see the nation state as stemming from nationalism'.[17] The only problem with such claims is that they run counter to all the facts.

The nation state has continued obstinately to reassert itself, not in spasmodic death throes, but with an increasing regularity, confidence and vigour. Whereas a number of voices in the 1990s predicted a gradual progression to transnational forms of government, the subsequent twenty years showed the opposite trend, from the breakup of the Soviet Union and the fragmentation of Yugoslavia, to a resurgence of independence movements across Europe, Africa, central Asia, the Middle East and South America. People seem to desire smaller units of government, not larger; national not transnational. In 1950 there were 100 internationally recognised sovereign states, today there are 195. In economic terms, nation states (and particularly small nation states) continually outperform large federations and empires.[18] History is proving the transnationalists to be demonstrably misguided.

The American Economist Pankaj Ghemawat enumerates numerous facts which contradict the view that globalisation has overturned the primacy of the nation state. International phone calls comprise about 3 per cent of global calls, cross border investment constitutes only around 10 per cent of total global investment and international students make up only 2% of the global student population.[19] While international trade may be more globalised (as it has been for several hundred years), this does not serve to erode the sense of national identity felt by the average man or woman; rather, goods and services just adopt a novel localised form, which eventually becomes part of the culture, tea being the most frequently cited nineteenth century example of this phenomenon. Ghemawat has termed the myth of globalisation, globaloney.[20]

There will remain those, like Bertrand Russell, who point to the international conflicts that have plagued continents and claim that national identity is merely a tribal identity writ large, and therefore opens the possibility of titanic conflict on the world stage. Yet, there is good reason to doubt that banishing the nation state would diminish human conflict.

Conflict is symptomatic of human nature, not of nation states.
Whatever form of community humanity adopts, there will always remain the possibility and indeed the likelihood of conflict. The great moral achievement of the nation state is that such conflict is effectively restrained within a nation's internal borders, rendered less viable by an effective system of law and order and less likely due to shared values. Within a nation, community is not defined according to the arbitrary trivialities of skin colour, ethnicity or any of the other capricious biological factors that have divided humanity throughout its history. Rather, it is defined according to the broad consensus of moral values which are the lifeblood of a successful civilisation.

Summary
Nations allow bodies of people to transcend their tribal instincts and work together, collectively forming a national community, centred upon shared values, ideas and cultural customs. In doing so, nations allow us to buy into a grand project, in which we corporately share cultural norms and values. For this reason, nations facilitate democracy. All of this brings us to our next chapter. I have argued that nation states are uniquely conducive to the existence of stable social order. It is in this context that we are free to pursue our material and personal enrichment as human beings.

Chapter Three

THE MARKET

The inherent vice of capitalism is the unequal sharing of blessings;
the inherent virtue of socialism is the equal sharing of miseries –

Winston Churchill

In a 2017 speech Jeremy Corbyn spoke of the 'failed model of capitalism'. His views are increasingly popular with a generation who have grown up in the wake of the financial crisis, driven by rampant corporate greed and irresponsible spending. Despite the financial crash taking place after a decade of labour government, the Conservative Party has repeatedly been characterised as the 'nasty' party, composed of wealthy aristocrats and bankers, who sneer at the poor and engorge themselves at the expense of others. As Gordon Brown once put it, the Conservative party has pursued a 'crude free-market ideology based on the narrow pursuit of self interest'. These are charges that conservatives have done too little to repudiate. The result is that this narrative has inveigled a generation of young people into support for socialism.

There is an undeniably strong historical connection between conservatism and free markets. After meeting Adam Smith, the father of free market economics, Edmund Burke wrote that he was the 'only man who... thought on these topics exactly as I do'. Since that time, conservatives have generally been in favour of markets, domestically and internationally, from Robert Peel's repeal of the Corn Laws in the nineteenth century to Margaret Thatcher's denationalisation of British industry and deregulation of markets in the 1980s.

In this chapter I will make the case that the conservative belief in markets is not just a utilitarian desire to maximise profit, but that it is also a moral belief in the material and social goods that markets bring to our society. More significantly it emerges from the conservative belief in human freedom.

As we will see in the next chapter, we must be as careful and precise as possible when we use terminology such as 'freedom'. Too often the casual employment of this term has served as a catch all phrase for any self-serving enterprise operating at the expense of others. There is a crude conception of freedom, which is libertarian and commends the absolute unfettered good of the free market. By contrast, there is a more sophisticated conception of freedom, which commends markets, but with very clear caveats. Just as absolute social freedom (anarchy) must be circumscribed by law, so absolute economic freedom (neoliberalism) must be curtailed by clear moral imperatives and enforced by law. In this chapter we will first look at how markets engender personal and social freedom, which in turn maximises the possibility of civic virtue.

The virtue of markets
Markets are a positive force in society, which allow humans to prosper if they have something useful to offer the community. Modern history has clearly demonstrated this principle. Despite the Soviet Union's optimism in a state-run command economy, it was comprehensively outperformed by the USA between the end of WW2 and the eventual collapse of the Soviet Union in the early 1990s. By 1989 the Soviet Union's GDP was $2,500 billion, compared with the USA's $4,862 billion. By 1990 GDP per capita in the Soviet Union was $9,211 compared with $21,082 in the USA. As the Russian economist Grigory Yavlinksy put it during the Cold War 'the Soviet system is not working because the workers are not working'.

Ironically, the early Soviet economic system was little more than modern feudalism. Marx's doctrines had released the peasants from their old masters' estates and driven them into their new masters' factories. The state provided enough goods and capital for subsistence and in return the people laboured for the state. Such an equation provides very little incentive for creativity, hard work or competition. The effect of constantly looking to the state, as opposed to one's fellow citizens, also had a harrowing effect on the moral character of the nation.[21] By contrast, the American economy promised reward to those who were willing to advance their own fortunes and, since people did not simply look to the state as the provider of all their needs, it encouraged a culture of innovation and strong civic engagement.[22]

In East and West Germany we find the same stark example of a state run economy competing against a capitalist economy. In 1991 GDP per capita in Soviet controlled East Germany was less than half of that in West Germany. The number of private households with heating was at 60% in East Germany, compared with 90% in West Germany. Levels of happiness were also higher when surveyed in West Germany.[23] Perhaps, the most striking contrast we can see between a state-run economy and a capitalist economy is that of North Korea and South Korea. According to figures from 2013, South Korea has a GDP of $1.19 trillion, compared with North Korea's $33 billion. In per capita terms this equates to a staggering disparity of $33,200 in the South compared with a meagre $1,800 in the North.

In the last few years one of the most egregious examples of the destructive power of state run socialism has been on display in what was once the richest country in South America, Venezuela. Jeremy Corbyn, John McDonnell and other key figures of the modern labour party are great admirers of the late Hugo Chavez, Venezuela's socialist former leader.

Chavez became president in 1998 and pioneered the redistribution of wealth in the country. The economy was closely regulated and run by the state. Chavez nationalised all major businesses and introduced price controls on goods, while propping the economy up with foreign loans and oil resources, which are some of the largest in the world. But over the course of ten years his policies bore toxic fruit; the result has been catastrophic for the Venezuelan people.

By 2013 inflation was at a shocking 50%, increasing dramatically the following year. By late 2018 the nation was in free fall, inflation running at an almost inconceivable 1,370,000%. The government was unable to print money, the people were starving and lacked even basic amenities, many were forced to scavenge from bins and malaria levels rocketed; unsurprisingly, refugees poured out of the country into Colombia and Brazil.

As in most socialist nations, Chavez and his successor Nicolás Maduro held on to power through intimidation, violence, arbitrary detentions and the repression of free speech. In 2018 Nicolás Maduro was seen eating steak at a top restaurant in Istanbul, while his countrymen literally starved. The socialist economic policies that led to this spiralling descent were lauded by the leaders of the British Labour Party. They are policies that have never failed to result in human misery every time they have been implemented. The important question we must ask is why?

In *The Wealth of Nations* Adam Smith gave the first and most enduring account of the free market. He postulated that 'It is not from the benevolence of the butcher, the brewer, or the baker that we expect our dinner, but from their regard to their own interest. We address ourselves not to their humanity but to their self-love.'[24] The key to the economic success of capitalist nations is that they harness the potential of anyone who wishes to improve their own lot. The magic of Smith's invisible hand is that, in improving their own lot, the hard-working butcher, brewer, or baker generally improves the common lot by providing a useful service to customers and employment to a workforce. In this way the capitalist state is propelled forward by the twin motors of private ownership and competition. By contrast, the socialist state is centralised, unresponsive to consumer demand and it lacks incentives to work. In truth, the cold war was not only a race between two states, but also between government apparatchiks and millions of American entrepreneurs. There was only ever going to be one winner; the Cold War was not won by the American State, but by the American worker.

For many, capitalism has connotations of self-serving greed, while communism has the more laudable aspiration of transcending self-interest for the common good. The first thing to say in response is that the conservative tradition is premised on a basic realism (and humility) about human nature. As benevolent as the intentions of some communists may be, the shortcomings of human nature have undermined every attempt of those elevating a socialist ideology that subjugates individuals in the service of a higher ideal. We are not all saints and any ideology which is built upon this axiom will inevitably founder. Yet, neither is human nature entirely dissolute. The genius of capitalism is that it channels the mixed motivations of human nature, driving our best and worst instincts towards the same ends for the common good. The economic success of a system does not necessarily make it right, so I will offer four reasons why the capitalist system of (generally) free markets is not only more prosperous than the state run economies of socialist regimes, but more virtuous.

Firstly, and most obviously, free market capitalism ensures that, in general, the wellbeing of the baker is conjoined to the common wellbeing of the community. If the baker is to be paid, he must provide a service that is valued by his community more broadly. In a competitive marketplace, the quality of his service and the affordability of his goods will be directly correlated to his own profits. By contrast, a state-run economy with no competition will have little incentive to provide a good service or make it affordable. Moreover, there are broader social goods which come from businesses whose profits rest on their reputation. In the sixteenth century, the Dominican friar Tomás de Mercado observed that privately owned property in Seville was in good keeping, whereas council property was constantly in disrepair; he concluded 'If universal love won't induce people to take care of things, private interest will'.[25] In the case of our baker, his profits will also be dependent on the manner in which he interacts with his customers, how hard he works and other such factors that are likely to produce positive social effects.

Secondly, the self-interest of the baker need not be the *sole* motive for his work. As Adam Smith himself pointed out:

> How selfish so ever man may be supposed, there are evidently some principles in his nature which interest him in the fortune of others, and render their happiness necessary to him, though he derives nothing from it except the pleasure of seeing it.[26]

There are a host of factors which motivate us in our work and, for many people, the maximisation of earnings is secondary to helping others, or doing something they enjoy. To return to Smith's example of the baker, perhaps the baker was raised by a father who was also a baker and his work makes him feel connected to his family tradition. Perhaps he takes great satisfaction in seeing his customers enjoying his daily produce and relishes his reputation as the best baker in the region. As long as he can make a reasonable living and provide for his family, these factors are enough to keep him very contented in his trade, despite the fact that more profitable trades are viable career choices in his area.

The key point is that, in capitalist economies, individuals are free to pursue their own choice of work for whatever reason they choose. This is a good thing for the development of skill and character, but above all personal satisfaction. Given that we spend much of our lives at work, a command economy which forces individuals into jobs for which they do not have any aptitude or passion is both inefficient and wasteful of human talent. There are myriad factors which motivate people to engage in a certain type of work, and it is therefore wrong to see greed as the root of capitalism. The root of work in a capitalist economy is as diverse and idiosyncratic as the spectrum of human motivations. Statistically, a sense of meaningful work is a key element in contributing to human happiness.[27] It is therefore important that we allow people to channel their passions, as it both benefits them and their society.

Thirdly, the baker who serves his community well will very likely end up with a healthy level of disposable income. He is then in the fortunate position of using that income to invest in any cause that he deems virtuous or worthwhile. He may invest it in a company that he thinks will return a profit, he may give the money to charity, or he may simply spend it on himself and his own family. In each of these cases the possibility for civic work and moral self development are present. Virtue, in the capitalist economy, is exercised by free choice in the private sphere, not by compulsion in the public sphere. Free choice is the precondition of virtue, as virtue under compulsion is no virtue at all. It is the capitalist system that opens up the greater possibility for moral reflection, as not only is wealth capable of being used instrumentally for the personal pursuit of good, but capitalism permits individuals to pursue a line of work in keeping with their ideals, without forcing them to do so.[28]

Fourthly, capitalism is premised on the freedom of civil association. A capitalist system can only work in a nation that allows individuals to assess their own needs and engage in voluntary transactions with other citizens. Not only does this forge the ties of association which are the sinews of the social body, but it engenders a robust civil freedom. A capitalist nation that tries to suppress the power of free association will soon find itself opposed by a vast amount of wealth and political interest. By contrast, command economies place vast amounts of power in the hands of a very few. As the historian Lord Acton pointed out, 'power corrupts and absolute power corrupts absolutely'. As a general principle the extension of economic power to millions of stakeholders helps to bulwark a society against tyranny.

Markets and limited government
In 301 AD the Emperor Diocletian issued an Edict Concerning the Sale Price of Goods. From his throne in Antioch he decreed a maximum price for over a thousand goods. Yet, for all the authority of a Roman potentate, his diktat was ignored. In 2013 the Labour leader Ed Miliband proposed a freeze on gas and electricity bills for twenty months, if he was elected. The Emperor Diocletian and Ed Miliband may not have much in common, but in this mistake they were united. Neither considered the perverse effects that tampering with the market value of goods and services can cause.

In his 'invisible hand' argument Smith demonstrated that the laws of supply and demand are what determine the value of goods. The free market then allows goods to reach an equilibrium determined by human valuation which is enforced by effective competition. This is not an infallible method of price setting, not least because human perception of value can be distorted.[29] Nevertheless, it provides the best solution for the fair valuation of goods and services, which will benefit the consumer and the service provider. This process largely keeps the government out of the business of price setting.

Fixing the price of goods or services at a lower rate than their market value means that businesses become less profitable. This disincentivises both external and internal investment, which makes businesses less efficient and further reduces competition. In the long run this will either drive up prices in an effort to recoup profits or result in a collapse of the provision of service. Either way, the most effective means of price regulation is the competition between service providers, which, given an effective market, will incentivise a fair price and a good service.

It is not just in the regulation of prices that big government is simply outperformed by the 'hive' mind of the market. Alexis de Tocqueville noted that the French had an almost unbounded confidence in the abilities of a big government to match the productivity of American associations. In this matter, Tocqueville argued, 'they are mistaken'. He questioned, 'what political power could ever carry on the vast multitude of lesser undertakings which the American citizens perform every day, with the assistance of the principle of association?'[30] It is a question which has never been answered.

Tocqueville anticipated that in the modern world the burden of care for citizens would increasingly fall on governments. He predicted that 'The task of the governing power will therefore perpetually increase'. Rhetorically, he questioned:

> Will the administration of the country ultimately assume the management of all the manufacturers, which no single citizen is able to carry on?... The morals and the intelligence of a democratic people would be as much endangered as its business and manufactures, if the government ever wholly usurped the place of private companies.[31]

In such passages Tocqueville seems to anticipate the gargantuan bureaucracy of future states, most obviously the communist regimes of the twentieth century. Rightly, he anticipated their failure.

In 1966 only 3% of sown land in the USSR was privately owned. Yet this 3% was responsible for a vast and disproportionate amount of Soviet agricultural production (64% of USSR potato production, 43% of vegetable production, 40% of meat production and 66% of egg production). When Nikita Khrushchev attempted to curtail private farming in 1958 there was a rapid contraction of agricultural produce (40% in eggs, milk and meat, 30% in potatoes and poultry, 26% in vegetables) and his policy was subsequently revoked. [32] A belief in markets is not just a matter of economic preference, it is a moral question. Communism's ideological opposition to markets led to millions suffering and dying from starvation in both the Soviet Union and China during the course of the twentieth century.

The conservative critique of big government's ability to create wealth has continued ever since the time of Tocqueville. Yet, it is important not to demonise government *per se*. When we speak of 'government' in such terms, it is easy for it to be reified into a monstrous phantasm. The reality is that, without government, businesses would fail. Governments provide laws and large scale infrastructure, they defend intellectual property rights, they prevent or regulate monopolies, they protect the environment and, most fundamentally, they ensure a stable and law abiding society in which businesses can flourish. But they can only do this when they govern with a light touch, create comprehensible laws and seek to help business rather than stifle and supplant it.

In 2017 the British Labour party fought an uncompromisingly left wing political campaign. They promised to spend billions renationalising industries while paying for thousands more police officers, nurses and doctors. They promised students that they would end tuition fees, give young people a free education and increase housing benefits at the same time as increasing pensions. It sounds too good to be true – and unfortunately it is. Many of the first-time labour voters were too young to remember the last time Britain pursued these policies. Those who remembered the strikes, stagflation, high taxes and paralysis of the UK economy in the 1970s may have been more reticent about the promised land of socialism that Jeremy Corbyn held out to his hopeful young followers. The simple question that was asked by his critics was 'who is paying for all of this?'

The answer, of course, is the British taxpayer. The most commonly employed weapon of the socialist's arsenal is caricature. Labour voters were led to envisage a modern-day Marie Antoinette, sat in her manor house scoffing at the poor. Surely, many asked, is it not these people who should be stripped of their extravagances, to provide for the deserving poor? Yet the reality is very different. It is the hard working shop owner, who has big dreams for their children, that is hit hardest by socialism.

Why big government isn't a solution
We have looked at why private enterprise incentivises hard work, rewards efficiency and often leads to greater productivity. It is therefore no surprise that the private sector is often a more effective service provider than the public sector.[33] There are clearly areas of public life where it is appropriate for the government to provide public goods, areas in which markets will fail to adequately resource public life, but whenever possible it is desirable to limit government intervention.

The first reason for this is because every pound spent by the government diverts money from the productive private sector. When Jeremy Corbyn says that he wants to 'bring energy, rail, water, and mail into public ownership', he doesn't acknowledge that this is billions of pounds of money which would be sucked into the inefficient bureaucracy of public services. As Theresa May pointed out on Question Time in 2017, 'there is no magic money tree'. An indignant Guardian columnist wrote an article riposting that 'of course there is a magic money tree'.[34] So, where does the government get this money from?

One option open to governments is to borrow money from domestic investors in the form of bonds, or to simply take money from citizens as taxes. However, this transfers money from the private sector (where it would otherwise be spent on businesses or invested in wealth creation), to the public sector, thereby eroding the more productive part of the economy. Either way, no new wealth is being created in this transaction and this option is likely to slow growth. The socialist belief in radically redistributing wealth through extremely high taxes is based on the false assumption that the money the rich possess is directly related to the poverty of the poor; as if the rich got rich by taking the poor's rightful allocation of money. Given a moment's reflection, this is not a tenable belief. Henry Ford didn't become rich by stealing money from the poor. He became rich because he had the passion to innovate a new motor car and the genius to mass manufacture it using new production methods. This process created wealth (in the form of cars) where there was no wealth before; people were willing to pay to possess this form of wealth, making their lives richer and simultaneously making Henry Ford richer. In the longer term this also had the additional effect of creating thousands of jobs, thereby distributing the newly created wealth and investing in the nation in the form of taxes. This is not to say that CEOs shouldn't pay a fair wage to employees, but without such entrepreneurs the poor would not be any richer; in fact they would be a lot less well off as there would not be wealth creators to pay the taxes which support the poorest.

Another option open to governments is to borrow money externally, whether from foreign banks or international organisations such as the IMF. However, if the UK borrows money from other nations, it must be done in sterling denominated currency. Therefore, for other nations to buy UK bonds, the UK must either invest money abroad, acquire goods or services from foreign nations, or exchange UK money for foreign currency. Either way these options take sterling out of circulation in the UK, thereby creating an opportunity cost equal to the amount that is being borrowed. No new money is being added to the UK economy as the balance of trade remains unchanged. It also has the adverse effect of creating large interest payments, meaning that money which could be used productively is simply sent abroad to be used by foreign governments. As a nation's level of debt increases the government will usually have to sell bonds at a lower price for higher yields, creating a vicious cycle. This was a conundrum that destroyed the public finances of Greece and Ireland in the darkest days of the 2011-12 eurozone crisis.

The final option is a Central Bank which can print more money.[35] We shall see that sometimes this option is a necessity to help provide liquidity for the economy. In 1957 the Conservative Prime Minister Harold Macmillan pursued a programme of government stimulus, accompanied by tax cuts and pro-market policies, following a run on the pound prompted by the Suez Crisis and a recession in 1956. This policy proved to be a relative success in the short term. Yet outside of a recession, the obvious problem with printing more money is that if there is twice as much money in circulation, then everything will cost twice as much – a phenomenon otherwise known as inflation. The resulting increase in the nominal size of the economy is illusory. No new goods or services have been created and no real value has been added to the economy; output has remained unchanged.

The more sinister side effect of this solution is that doubling the currency in circulation will simultaneously halve the value of the existing currency. In doing so it penalises savers for being financially responsible. In history's most extreme examples a lifetime of savings have been wiped out, such as in Weimar Germany following World War I. The value of a German Mark fell from 4.2 to the dollar in 1914 to 4.2 trillion to the dollar by late 1923. The economist Milton Friedman said 'inflation is taxation without legislation'. In other words, it is a means of robbing a person's savings without ever opening the vault. While a degree of inflation is generally considered necessary to stave off deflation and increase aggregate demand, this is usually maintained at a very low annual rate; the Federal Reserve favours 2%.

All of the options for generating public money have a strong propensity to make the economy less productive. The secondary effect is less prosperity and fewer jobs. In order to make up the economic shortfall governments often look to greater taxation, thereby exacerbating the problem. The result is a vicious cycle, in which public spending begets ever more public spending.

More dangerously, this creates a public mentality which sees government as the remedy to all problems. As public spending increases and becomes the norm, it is very easy to automatically look to government when a problem arises. Rather than addressing issues through our own communal efforts, we look to a faceless entity with seemingly unlimited funds at its disposal, which has no link in the public imagination to the hard work and taxes of our fellow citizens. Such an approach dispossesses us of the responsibility for our own society.

Jeremy Corbyn is openly contemptuous of capitalism. His brand of socialism seeks to wrap the coils of state bureaucracy around the market. In de-oxygenating the productive part of the economy, the whole nation suffers. This is a lesson Francois Hollande, the socialist President of France, learned the hard way when he introduced a 75% top level of tax in 2012. By 2015 it was obvious that the tax had failed. It hadn't raised anywhere near its anticipated income for the government and many wealthy French businessmen fled abroad. As Margaret Thatcher put it, socialists would 'rather the poor were poorer, provided the rich were less rich'. It is the reason that socialism is sometimes called 'the politics of envy'.

Before moving on, we should add one crucial caveat to the case against big government. I have stressed throughout this book that conservatism is a common sense philosophy which acts rationally and not ideologically. In economics it is important that we are not blinded to the right choice in certain circumstances by an ideological attachment to the default conservative position. Economics is not a science and government spending does not always correlate to inefficiency. We have looked at principles which will generally hold true, but they are not laws of physics. To illustrate this point we might note two examples in which exceptional circumstances throw our general principles out of kilter.

We have seen that following the 2008 financial crisis the Greek and Irish government debt suffered soaring bond yields. In Britain, the Bank of England embarked on a programme of quantitative easing. This was to counter the deflationary pressure of the recession, and avoid the nation falling into a liquidity trap. In this instance, a sensible level of induced inflation was the right option under the circumstances. In contrast to Greece and Ireland, UK government bond yields decreased despite burgeoning levels of national debt. This was due to a strong international desire for secure investments, confidence in the UK market and the fact the UK government held a substantial proportion of its own debt. This does not mean that debt is good but it illustrates that, in economics, context is crucial.

The second example is even more striking. Japan had a staggering government debt level of 253% of GDP in 2017, almost 2.5 times that of the United States. While Greece's 2015 debt level of 177% plunged it into crisis, Japan has been relatively unaffected, maintaining a high credit rating and low bond yields. The reason for this is that Japan has a sovereign portfolio of valuable assets and most of their debt is held by domestic investors, which reassures international markets.

These examples illustrate that contingent factors can cause markets to react very differently in one set of circumstances to another. The simple point is that economic principles should generally be adhered to but, as non-ideological thinkers, conservatives ought to look at the circumstances surrounding each economic question and not pursue a party line dogmatically irrespective of the facts. In all political questions, the straight lines of abstract theory must yield to the gravity of circumstance.

The moral limits of markets
So far we have looked at how markets are a vital component to a free and prosperous society. Yet what happens when markets are left unregulated? We have already seen that, in political and economic theory, most absolute truths stand with the crutch of a caveat. The truth that the market is a good thing is no exception. There are those who see the unfettered free market as an unqualified social good and make an ideology out of it. Such a view is mistaken.

Modern economics is premised on the idea of the rational individual. It is only working with this assumption that economists can employ mathematical models of how the economy (which is driven by human behaviour) will react. This strain of economics follows the rationalist liberals of the eighteenth century who, inspired by the equations of Newtonian physics, tried to create the ideal society based on the idea that humans are rational, predictable beings. Needless to say their experiment failed magnificently, leading to bloodshed and autocracy in the late eighteenth century. As the ancient Greeks identified over two thousand years ago, politics and economics are not sciences to which we can apply formulas; they are humanities, with all the ambiguity and unpredictability which that entails.

In 2002 the Nobel Prize for economics was awarded to Daniel Kahneman and Amos Tversky. The argument of their work was that human behaviour is not rational in the way that the predictive model of economics assumes it to be. According to their work, the heuristic assumptions of humans are often incorrect, rendering many of our choices, including economic choices, wrong. George Akerlof and Robert Shiller authored *Animal Spirits,* a term they appropriated from John Maynard Keynes, showing that human psychology and emotion are the fundamental driving forces behind the economy.[36] In other words, the models of neo-classical economics, which see humans as rational creatures who are liable to make informed and sensible decisions, are fundamentally flawed.

All of this is important because a belief in the fundamental rationality of human behaviour led to the belief that markets are rational and predictable entities. Alan Greenspan, the head of the Federal Reserve for three decades, famously articulated such a faith in deregulated markets. During his tenure he consistently opposed the regulation of markets, in particular the regulation of the sort of financial derivatives which led to the global economic crisis in 2008. What Greenspan and others did not account for was an understanding of flawed human beings which was taken for granted until the middle of the twentieth century. As Keynes is alleged to have remarked 'There is nothing so disastrous as a rational investment policy in an irrational world'.

The thing that neoliberalism missed was precisely the same thing that socialism missed: human nature. Where the neoliberals assumed that human nature was rational, the socialists assumed that human nature was benign. Both systems have resulted in failure because they did not introduce the checks, balances and diffusion of power which are necessary to govern human nature as it actually is: limited in perspective and flawed. The historically Christian account of humans, as beings capable of great good but also capable of great evil, had been usurped by a self confidence in human rationality. The results nearly led to a global financial collapse.

Not only should the market be mindful of human nature, but it is also right that there should be other limits on the market. Economic prosperity is important, but it is not everything. It must be weighed against a number of other social goods operative in the life of a nation: human flourishing, cultural identity, national security, compassionate care for the sick and the protection of the natural and historical environment. In Britain, the Financial Conduct Authority has endeavoured to ensure that the banks never act so irresponsibly with taxpayers' money again. Simple measures such as capital requirements to prevent bank insolvency or mandatory disclosure of a bank's finances to government agencies are a necessary step to prevent a repetition of 2008. When a bank the size of RBS fails, it is everyday people who suffer; this simple fact makes their business the business of us all.

Rather than taking the socialist line, which throws the baby out with the bathwater, the conservative tradition takes the common-sense approach and acknowledges that markets are a genuine good in our society. They bring prosperity, create connections and instil community. But they have their flaws, because they are a product of human decisions. These flaws must be mitigated and not magnified. The great challenge of capitalism is to welcome economic vitality without worshipping material wealth. Economic policies must always have the interests the people at their heart. This does not mean choosing economic redistribution by the big state. It means making sure that capitalism is able to bring opportunity to every person with big dreams, just as it does to the privileged.

This acknowledgement has significant precedent among conservative leaders. In 1904 the Republican Theodore Roosevelt campaigned on the pledge of delivering a 'Square Deal' to the people of the United States. He offered a package of reforms, which included reform of industry and business practices, where monopolists were exploiting their power. Roosevelt pointed out that it was inconceivable that 'free people will permanently tolerate the vast power conferred by vast wealth... without lodging somewhere in government the still higher power of seeing that this power is used for and not against the interests of the people as a whole'. In 1905 he said 'somehow or other, we should have to work out methods of controlling the big corporations without paralysing the energies of the business community'. Roosevelt was a Republican who angered some of the industrial magnates of his day in order to deliver vital reforms. Today this middle road of socially conscious conservatism must be pursued again.

The truth that Roosevelt realised is that capitalism requires law. This is not about the proliferation of red tape, but the provision of healthy market conditions. Low barriers to entry for small businesses help to create competition and break up the oligopolies of companies which dominate some sectors of the market. Regulating businesses and enforcing antitrust laws ensure that growth is sustainable and citizens are not collateral damage to the interests of the richest. Closing tax loopholes means that people pay their fair share into the common pot. Raising penalties (such as the Immigration Skills Charge) for unfair employment models ensures that businesses do not undercut local labour forces, thereby artificially undermining a sustainable living wage. When we look in detail at the reality of a capitalist economy, the apparent opposition of capitalism to government intervention is not so stark. A limited level of government regulation is a crucial framework for a competitive marketplace.[37] Without such oversight the ecosystem of the market can become dominated by the biggest beasts and cease to serve the public interest.

There is therefore a symbiosis between limited government and healthy capitalism. With the admission that the funding of the public sector is contingent upon the flourishing of the private sector, we can come to sensible conclusions about the extent to which the state wishes to burden the private sector with taxes for the promotion of shared public goods. This cannot be formulaic and will be contingent upon the needs of a given state.

Investing large amounts of money in state education or healthcare does not automatically translate into good results or healthy institutions. The key lies in building *effective* institutions. Taken together, limited government, effective institutions and the great engines of capitalism, will prove a formidable recipe for economic growth *at all levels of society*.

We have already looked at how, domestically, we might maintain a healthy private sector which is able to fund the public sector, but how can we keep our economy competitive on an international stage? From a moral perspective we must also ask the question as to whether there is a means of international trade which emulates the benign effect of domestic markets. That is, does the market principle, that both parties can be winners, also apply on the international stage?

Free Trade and Protectionism
Between 1815 and 1846 Great Britain shielded the domestic production of grain from international markets by introducing heavy tariffs on imports. These measures were in large part a response to the burgeoning agricultural industries of the United States and Russia. Britain was not alone in introducing tariffs; it was a decision mirrored by almost every continental power across the English Channel. The introduction of these tariffs sparked a debate which has raged to this day.

On one side of the debate liberals such as Richard Cobden passionately argued that the repeal of the Corn Laws would bring cheap food to the poor, increase the trading opportunities for manufacturers and diminish the power of the landlords. Cobden and his fellow advocates, utilising the arguments for free trade advocated by the economist David Ricardo, made the case that it would lead to greater overall wealth. Cheap imports of bread would lead to cheaper bread, which would leave more money in the pocket of workers. The hope was that this would lead to investment of that surplus money in clothes, thus enriching manufacturers, leading to greater employment and greater national prosperity.

On the other side of the debate the two leading advocates against the repeal of the Corn Laws were Benjamin Disraeli and Lord Bentick. The arguments of Disraeli and Bentick were based on the belief that there were more fundamental social issues at stake than the cost of food. It is true that Disraeli wanted to shepherd the interests of the British landowners, many of who were stalwart Tories – Lord Bentick led this faction. But, if we look at Disraeli's key arguments they are centred on the belief that opening the doors to cheap foreign imports would decimate the agricultural labour force of Britain. In Parliament he inveighed:

> this is not a question of rent, but it is a question of displacing the labour of England that produces corn, in order, on an extensive and even universal scale, to permit the entrance into this country of foreign corn produced by foreign labour. Will that displaced labour find new employment?'

His other key concern was enriching Britain's enemies and thereby jeopardising British security, all for the short term gain of cheaper grain. He finished his peroration with a warning that there would be 'an awakening of bitterness' after the 'midnight of [the free trade proponents'] intoxication'. He warns against the 'depraved desire that the rich may become richer without the interference of industry and toil', urging the people to 'return to those principles that made England great... the cause of labour – the cause of the people – the cause of England.'

Such speeches resonated with large swathes of the population and prompted a number of other concerns which were given voice in public meetings and newspapers. One concern raised in *The Spectator* in 1843 points out that other public goods would suffer as a result of the severance of a national industry:

> A reduction of corn-rents must throw land out of cultivation, destroy capital invested in the cultivation of inferior soils, and lower the wages of agricultural labour by diminishing the demand for it: farmers become insolvent.[38]

The same writer also questions what would happen if a foreign power should impose tariffs or cease to export. Such a country would have enormous leverage over Britain and could reduce it to famine.

The impact on the countryside was indeed devastating. At the close of the nineteenth century British farming was a pale shadow of its former prosperity and the employment of males in agricultural professions had diminished by a third. [39] It is unsurprising that the issue ultimately split the conservative party in two. The majority of the conservatives followed Bentick to form the New Conservative Party, while around one hundred followed Peel to form the Liberal Party. Over 150 years later, the issue continues to divide opinion. The historian A.N. Wilson points at the huge unemployment and loss of agricultural land which resulted from the exposure of British agriculture to international markets. He writes:

> Only industrialised Britain and Belgium chose to believe Cobden's discredited dogma that commercial intercourse between nations inevitably spells progress... By 1885, the British area under wheat had shrunk by a million acres. By the 1880s the British were importing an absurd 65 per cent of their wheat, and nearly a million workers had left the land.[40]

Between 1871 and 1881 there was a decline of 92,250 agricultural labourers. Britain simply could not compete with the mechanised prairies of America, and the serf driven plains of Russia. Relinquishing its role as the world's great agricultural nation, Britain shifted its focus towards industry. The issue was not to be decisively resolved within the Conservative Party and rumbled on, almost splitting the Party in the 1890s, when Arthur Balfour and Joseph Chamberlain came to loggerheads over the issue.

A century later a similar debate was to be played out again in the 1980s. This time industry was being replaced by the burgeoning services sector. In 1846 Disraeli asked parliament 'what are the resources that would furnish employment to two-thirds of the subverted agricultural population – in fact, from 3,500,000 to 4,000,000 of the people?'. Similar concerns were echoed at the 1984 Labour Party Conference. The party leader Neil Kinnock inveighed that the miners of South Wales 'know that pit closure would trap them, entomb them, in unemployment and deprivation for all the foreseeable future under Toryism'.[41] The irony was that this time it was a Conservative leader removing the insulation of tariffs and exposing British industry to the chastening winds of the international markets.

Thatcher was morally right to tackle the militant NUM and the 'enemy within' (its executive) who were predominantly Marxists with links to the USSR. She was economically right; the NCB was selling coal around 25% above international market prices. She was politically right; democracy was being subverted, the nation held hostage by the executive of the NUM whose methods and aims did not have public support.[42] She was right in saying that 'wages must be related to productivity'.[43] Yet, she was wrong in her absolute confidence in the market. The belief that unemployment would lead to competitive wages and attract investment in mining communities proved to be incorrect. Rather than the government subsidising industries which forged character and community, it would end up subsidising welfare dependency in deeply deprived areas. Given the context, Thatcher pursued the right policy, but did not do enough to mitigate the effects of such a rapid transition. This left a bitter scar in communities that needed the government to help actively channel market investment for the common good.

In 2018, the question remained as controversial and context dependent as ever. Donald Trump introduced a 25% tariff on steel from the European Union, Canada and Mexico, in the hope of reviving the American steel industry. Perhaps more significantly, Trump introduced a series of tariffs against China, covering several sectors from agriculture and industry to transport and energy. America has pedigree when it comes to protectionism. The Smoot-Hawley Tariff act of 1930 tariffed over 20,000 foreign imports in a bid to boost domestic production and consumption during the Great Depression. As the essayist Pankaj Mishra has pointed out, the most successful economies of the twentieth century, including America, Germany, Japan and China, did not always employ Milton Friedman's model of economic liberalism, but rather turned to the 'Hamiltonian Model' when it suited them, that is, the protection of nascent industries advocated by Alexander Hamilton, who observed this practice in eighteenth century Britain.[44] With the exponential rise of China driven by state subsidies, protectionist tariffs and currency manipulation, the late twentieth century consensus that economic liberalism constitutes 'The End of History' is beginning to look increasingly simplistic.

Indeed, it is not hard to see the logic behind some of Trump's claims. Since China's ascent to the WTO in 2001 it has run an increasingly titanic trade surplus with America, numbering literally hundreds of billions of dollars. This surplus has been achieved by a number of tactics, such as aggressively subsidising domestic industries and artificially devaluing the Chinese Yuan to boost exports. Their stratospheric ascent into economic dominance of the East has given China significant political leverage over the United States, not least because it has used its currency reserves to purchase a large proportion of US debt.

While liberal economists argue that free trade benefits everyone, this is usually based on the premise that the maximisation of individual choice is the ultimate good. In the real world, broader questions must be answered. Are cheap goods in Walmart really a desirable exchange for filling the vaults of China's treasury with American wealth? With an increasingly muscular Chinese military on the world stage, will we look back and think that this was a prudent long term strategy, or will we regret our short term thinking? Moreover, an advocacy of free trade is usually based on the assumption that we are trading with nations who also embrace free trade; this is the basic premise behind Ricardo's advocacy of comparative advantage. Yet China's malpractice has sought to outsmart the aspiration for global free trade, 'having their cake and eating it'. In an economic analogue of 'the prisoner's dilemma', it seems that sometimes a nation can achieve the most favourable outcome when everyone else plays by the rules except for them. If one weighs the evidence, Trump's claim, that the United States has been on the wrong end of a bad deal with China, seems justified.

The debate between free trade and protectionism will inevitably rumble on, especially within conservative circles. When a 2013 NatCen poll asked if Britain should limit the import of foreign products in order to protect its national economy, 48% of people agreed with the statement.[45] The most conservative response to such questions ought to be the least ideologically polarised and the most measured. We can say that the liberal dogma which treats free trade as a good in all places at all times is as faulty as the converse solution. The complex contours of such questions cannot be navigated by the pursuit of unwavering absolutes. They are contextually dependent and, as such, require prudence.

In the general course of international affairs it would seem self evident that trade with our friends and allies is a mutually beneficial arrangement. Yet, there will be times in a nation's life when a particular industry must be shielded from the squalls of international markets. There are also times when a nation must be wary of whom they are making rich. This was recognised by Joseph Chamberlain, the great advocate of tariffs in the 1890s, with his doctrine of Imperial Preference. Such considerations are in keeping with the primary duty of a nation, which is to protect its citizens. A conservative policy will seek to enrich its citizens beyond simply providing them with the cheapest commodities or the maximisation of choice; it will seek to provide them with the opportunity to pursue useful and enriching work.

The Abandonment of the Working Class

In modern Britain there is a clear consensus of anger and betrayal among the working class. There is a palpable disappointment at the economic stagnation that has continued under successive governments. The figures justify these claims. Real income dropped 10% in the six years after the financial crash, while they remained stagnant in real terms between 2003 and 2015. The result for working class communities has been inertia and a sense of hopelessness, particularly for young people, sixty per cent of who still live within twenty miles of where they lived aged fourteen.[46] Both the left and the right have too often left behind the working class Briton, pandering predominantly to the interests of the affluent middle class.

For this the Conservative Party must take some blame. We have seen that in the 1980s Margaret Thatcher boldly tackled militant unions like the NUM, which were led by Marxists such as Arthur Scargill and Michael McGahey. However, there was an assumption that the free market would automatically plug the gap left by the loss of 170 collieries and 171,000 miners. Margaret Thatcher believed that denationalisation would inevitably bring 'higher profits and rising investment'.[47] This claim may have been more credible if these industries had always been fully exposed to global markets and therefore declined more slowly. However, the result of the sudden withdrawal of state subsidies and removal of protective tariffs from these industries was that whole communities were left bereft.

This presented a contrast to other industrialised European nations where the transition into a service based economy was carefully managed. Nations such as Germany saw heavy expenditure on regionally targeted infrastructure and the retraining of workers to avoid the depression of industrial regions. To this day, former mining communities in areas such as South Wales and Teesside are economically depressed and welfare dependency remains high. The working class pride which defined these communities has been pitifully eroded.

The Conservative Party should have recognised that there was a value in these traditional working class communities, which needed to be nurtured alongside national economic growth. While Thatcher's Conservative government did focus on capital expenditure to aid economic growth, this had a national focus and was not sufficiently targeted at replacing the rapidly contracting industrial sector. For a party which is built on a belief in tradition, patriotism and the value of work, not enough was done to reinvent the ailing sense of identity of the working classes affected. It is no wonder that nearly all of these communities remain militantly anti-conservative. Yet, tragically, the left has adopted even more damaging policies for these communities over the last thirty years.

In the 1990s, Tony Blair's vision of a multicultural society opened the doors to mass immigration. The Blair government was so ideologically wedded to the idea of a multicultural society that they never considered the impact it was having on the communities they were supposed to be representing. By 2013, more than 75% of the population wanted immigration reduced, with 56 per cent of the population wanting it reduced a lot.[48]

Mass migration is a contentious issue in modern society, but it is one area where successive governments have failed to take account of the effect of their policies beyond the ostensible economic benefit. It may be easier for a government to allow foreign immigrants to provide a ready workforce that can afford to operate at a cheaper rate, but what of the social effects of such a policy on young British men and women who do not develop new skills or learn the discipline and gratification that can be found in work? In the long run, such policies are likely to prove costly, both on a human and an economic level. Simon Danczuk, a Labour MP, articulated this point well:

> Many of these job opportunities have all but disappeared to some working class Britons... I strongly believe my party should be forever beating a loud drum about the value of work, about instilling a strong work ethic into people and about how character and

achievement comes from hard work. My fear is that an increased reliance on cheap migrant labour to drive some sectors in our economy is chipping away at a bedrock of working class pride, allowing a once strong work ethic to drain away and its being done with a comfortable and badly misinformed political consensus.[49]

Creating employment opportunities for a nation's own citizens is part of a state's moral obligation to enrich the lives of its people. Enjoying the dignity of work is closely correlated to personal happiness. Conversely, being out of work has an array of negative repercussions, involving family life and mental health.[50] An examination of over three hundred studies on this subject showed that the number of unemployed people who experienced psychological problems was more than double that of those in employment. Depression and anxiety, in particular, were found to be significantly higher in the unemployed.[51] Such findings are a reflection of the fact that work has a transformative effect on individuals by bringing self worth, order and responsibility to their lives. The ripples of this effect are often felt in the whole community as people develop new skills, invest the money they have earned and contribute to the community of which they are part. Sadly, a society which values cheap labour above the development of character is far less likely to see value in creating work for its people.

While this may seem obvious to some there has too often been an unthinking condemnation of anyone who expresses concern over the free movement of people or mass immigration. As David Goodhart points out, there is a double standard in the moralising of liberals over the questions of mass immigration. The frustrations of working class Britons are often centred on 'a quest for meaning and collective identity in a secular, individualistic, economistic modern world. When people in Sunderland voted for Brexit apparently against their material interests it was considered stupid; when affluent people vote for higher taxes it is considered admirable.'[52]

There can be no doubt that immigrants to Britain have enriched our national life and our local communities. It is absolutely right that immigrants who want to make Britain their home should be welcomed. There is nevertheless a legitimate question as to the scale of such immigration. A number of studies have been conducted on the economic effects of mass immigration and there is certainly not a clear cut case for the unequivocal advantages of mass immigration. As the House of Lords Select Committee report on 'The Economic Impact of Immigration' states, 'The overall conclusion from existing evidence is that immigration has very small impacts on GDP per capita, whether these impacts are positive or negative'. It goes on to note that 'we found no systematic empirical evidence to suggest that net immigration creates significant dynamic benefit for the resident population in the UK... it is possible that there are also negative dynamic and wider welfare effects'.[53]

There is also clear evidence for the negative effects of mass immigration on poor communities. The House of Lords report states that 'immigration creates winners and losers in economic terms... The losers are likely to include those employed in low-paid jobs and directly competing with new immigrant workers.'[54] A study by the UCL Professor Christian Dustmann found 'wage competition and wage pressure at the low end of the wage distribution', concluding that 'the larger concern of the low-skilled population is, indeed, justified by the evidence'.[55] These findings go some way to explaining the deep anger that exists in some working class communities, who are often most proximate to the effects of mass immigration from incongruent cultures. It has been easy for metropolitan liberals to dismiss such grievances as simple bigotry.

Rather than accepting the cost of investing in young British people, employers, who benefit from cheap labour, understandably choose to employ a workforce of skilled overseas workers. Such a policy is good for the profits of businesses, but it is likely to be damaging for UK productivity in the long term; moreover it is damaging for the nations from which energetic young immigrants come. Yet this is often too difficult a subject for politicians to risk broaching. Elements of the political left have been so ideologically attracted to a cosmopolitan nation that they have wilfully ignored the plight of their own constituents. It is hard to see how this does not amount to moral cowardice and a failure of leadership. In 2018 Iain Duncan Smith, the chairman of the Centre for Social Justice, tackled this issue head on, calling for employers to invest in unemployed British workers.[56]

As a nation Britain must reassert the fact that we are not just citizens of the world, we are countrymen. As Stanley Baldwin said in 1926, 'That brotherhood which Conservatives and Unionists have among ourselves, and feel towards every class, will do far more to realise the ideals of our people than that preaching of class hatred which… returned the Labour Party to power'. We sleep soundly at night because our countrymen defend us overseas; we flourish because of the local communities and networks that we live in; we are cared for by organisations which are funded by the hard work and labour of our fellow citizens. It is right that a reciprocity and gratitude exists between us. Once a year, on Remembrance Sunday, we are vividly reminded of the bonds of unyielding loyalty which exist between countrymen. Yet, we are often quick to forget these deep ties of kinship in our everyday lives and our public policy. This unspoken contract between our fellow citizens, past, present and future must be restored in the public imagination. The stark truth is that it is all too easy for metropolitan middle income workers to show little empathy for the working class who fight their wars, pave their roads and build their houses. Going forward, we need to invest in our countrymen in a number of ways, not least through capital investment in impoverished areas, apprenticeships and a world class education system in the poorest parts of our country.[57]

Education

If Britain is going to be economically successful, then key to that success is investing in education. But more importantly, the creation of pathways out of poverty is a moral issue and should be recognised as such. In 1870 the Elementary Education Act was passed in Parliament. It was introduced to educate a rapidly democratising nation which also had increasing demand for innovation in its burgeoning industrial centres. These new schools were to be funded by local ratepayers (the nineteenth century equivalent of council tax). Thirty years later, the first British Prime Minister of the twentieth century, Arthur Balfour, realised that educational reform was still needed if Britain was to remain globally competitive; in particular the spectre of an increasingly educated and efficient German workforce haunted British politicians. In the 1902 Education Act, Balfour and his conservative government provided an increase in funds for education, which would be administered by local education authorities and made available to church schools. Despite its unpopularity with the liberals and nonconformists at the time, it meant that hundreds of schools for both boys and girls were opened.

Today, education remains a crucial area in which Britain has too often been behind the curve, compared to other major nations. In 1997 Tony Blair famously came to power with the mantra 'education, education, education'. His key aspiration for higher education was that half of all young people would go to university and earn a degree. Blair's legacy was that by 2015, 58.8 per cent of British graduates were working in a job that didn't require a degree. Blair had made the mistake of assuming that academic qualifications would create more jobs requiring them. In reality, the government should have provided clearly differentiated pathways to fill existing skills gaps in the labour market. In Germany, for example, the percentage of graduates was over twenty per cent lower, yet by offering higher quality university education to fewer individuals and offering a clear alternative of vocational training, their workforce has been the most effective in Europe. Key to a successful educational policy will be training young people for the skills that are needed in our market today, but also identifying the requisite skills for the market of tomorrow.

The former teacher Lucy Crehan travelled around five countries which had some of the highest PISA (OECD) scores in the world. She documented her observations from this journey in her book *Clever Lands*. Perhaps unsurprisingly, she concluded that there is no magic formula for educational success because a variety of factors make every country different. Yet she does identify some key principles. In these high performing countries she found very clear educational pathways to respected professions as well as a diversity of occupations to suit different types of intelligence, whether technical or academic.

She relates that 'Beyond 15, Finland, Japan, Shanghai and Singapore have separate vocational schools which specialise in various forms of technical and vocational education.'[58] In her view 'rather than solely focusing on getting students from poor backgrounds into university, we should ensure we provide excellent educational opportunities for those who choose not to go, whatever background they're from'.[59] This is a point that has been gradually recognised in Britain. In 2017, the British government announced that they wanted to see a 'genuine parity of esteem' between vocational and academic paths to employment. From 2019 T-Levels will be introduced, offering a clear route to technical employment which mirror A-Levels. The kinaesthetic intelligence that is required of technical work and manual labour is deserving of respect and investment, a fact that is rightly being acknowledged in our education system.

Crehan also points out the importance of cultural factors in relation to the success of educational outcomes. For instance, in Asian countries there was a strong sense that children did not take education for granted, but believed it to be a path to a better life. In China, there seems to be a deep rooted belief that with the right attitude anyone can achieve success, an idea that once characterised America. Similarly, in a country like Singapore the children have a deep seated respect for authority and an eagerness to learn that is cultivated in their family life. Their academic outcomes are unsurprisingly much better. In other words, while some educational systems are undoubtedly better than others, the culture of a nation is a decisive factor. Such observations affirm the conservative view that the culture nurtured by civil society brings an array of unforeseen social goods. A culture which prioritises the family and emphasises a healthy deference to authority may do more for Britain's ailing PISA rankings than any educational reform.

Finally, she makes the point that passionate teachers should not be intimidated by a sense of 'culpability and liability' while still insisting on 'responsibility'. In other words, we must trust our teachers and give them the professional freedom to teach in their own way, while still being answerable to a national curriculum. This principle can be applied to schools as much as it is applied to teachers. While Crehan does not make this link, the freedom and decentralisation of education is precisely what free schools hope to achieve, allowing communities to address their own needs in a decentralised fashion. As we have seen, the state is often far less effective than civil society at unlocking human potential. Fostering a participative ethos in society unleashes creativity and innovation. When free association is allowed to germinate, the result is a biodiversity of ideas and institutions.[60]

Free schools are simply state funded schools which are set up by voluntary groups – in some ways similar to the original model of British education in the nineteenth century. They have achieved notably better grades in national examinations than state run schools, both in the UK and in the USA.[61] Taken alongside private schools, the evidence indicates that the net result is a level of competition which forces higher standards and raises the bar across the board. In Niall Ferguson's Reith Lectures he addresses the fact that more choice in education leads to higher standards:

If you want to know one of the reasons why Asian teenagers do so much better than their British and American peers in standardised tests, it is this: private schools educate more than a quarter of pupils in Macao, Hong Kong, South Korea, Taiwan and Japan. The average PISA maths score for those places is ten per cent higher than for the UK and the U.S. The gap between them and us is as large as the gap between us and Turkey. And guess what? The share of Turkish students in private schools is below four per cent... more private education means higher quality and more efficient education for everyone.[62]

If this sounds similar to the operation of the market, that's because it is. The area between the private sector and the public sector is sometimes called the fourth sector, or social enterprise. Just as the market is driven by individuals who are passionate about the success of their business, civil society works because financial reward is not all that motivates humans. When human passion is unleashed in a whole range of areas, it will create innovation, an exchange of ideas, biodiversity and competition.

The conventional private sector also has a key part to play in equipping people with new skills. The Social Mobility Commission found that the Government only funds 7% of all investment in adult skills. Learning new skills is a lifelong process. If we are going to maximise the latent talents that people possess then they must have the opportunity to develop themselves after their formal education ends. The private sector encompasses everything from online courses to private tuition and employee training. It is important that the economic benefits of investing in employees are made clear to businesses; the end of formal education does not mean the end of the road for those who didn't excel at school.[63]

In education (and other areas of public life which are often monopolised by the government) it is the desire to create more choice and thereby raise standards for all citizens which motivates conservatives to expand the role of civil society. It is because conservatives can see that bureaucratised state institutions are failing the poorest in Britain that they are motivated to create *more choice*, not simply insist that all must be subject to equal poverty of choice. Equality in mediocrity will benefit no one. If socialist politicians wish to impose such mediocrity on the poorest, then who is really trampling on the disadvantaged?

Free schools alone are not a complete solution. We must empower teachers, cut red tape and become less fixated on results. But what is even more crucial to educational success is the culture that exists beyond the corridors of the school. As a nation we must rekindle a culture of aspiration and deference to legitimate authority. If strong values are inculcated in our families, then these will percolate into our classrooms, improving the prospects of students and enriching our society. Above all, we must not lose sight of the fact that it is a moral imperative incumbent on governments to create viable pathways out of poverty for those who wish to work.

The Welfare State

The British economist William Beveridge masterminded the welfare state in 1942, when he published a famous report called *Social Insurance and Allied Services*. When Clement Attlee's Labour government introduced the Welfare State in 1945, they did so in the expressed hope that the state would support the individual 'from the cradle to the grave'. Despite Beveridge's intention for the welfare state to provide a 'national minimum', leaving 'room and encouragement for voluntary action by each individual to provide more than that minimum for himself and his family', the welfare state experienced an astronomical inflation over the course of the next fifty years. The inflation adjusted figures for the increase in welfare provision are revealing. In 1948 welfare expenditure was, in modern terms, £11 billion. By 2012 it was almost twenty times greater at £200 billion. Even in the context of a growing GDP, this represents a significant increase from 4% to 13% of government expenditure relative to GDP. This trend was particularly significant in the first decade of the twenty first century. Between 2001 and 2015 welfare spending increased in real terms by £34 billion.

The central concern of conservatives who have seen the expansion of the welfare state is that it has not created freedom from poverty, but rather it has trapped the poorest in a dependency culture. Cash in hand benefits are at risk of being used to fund addictive habits such as gambling or drugs. Perversely, low paid work was actually disincentivised by the Labour government because it paid less than out of work benefits. Such a system is a certain way to keep the poor at the bottom of the social ladder. This is not a new conundrum in Britain. In 1832, the 'Royal Commission into the operation of the Poor Laws', found that the system of welfare was unsustainably expensive and was being abused by those who did not truly need it. As a result, the 1834 Poor Law Amendment Act was introduced to ensure that being in work paid more than claiming welfare from the state. While this Act was much maligned, not least in Dickensian novels, it represented the ever present tension between providing state aid to the poorest and trapping people in poverty by incentivising it.

The sensible middle ground of limited aid to the poorest in society was first championed by Benjamin Disraeli, who acknowledged that, at its most extreme, the *laissez faire* capitalism of the Benthamite utilitarians would forsake the disadvantaged. In Disraeli's novels, most notably *Sybil*, he emphasised the social obligations that the wealthy have to the poor, rejecting the individualistic society. His concern was that Britain would be riven into two nations: rich and poor.

The 'One Nation' ethos was picked up in the twentieth century by Stanley Baldwin. Baldwin was an industrialist with a strong Christian faith. He believed himself to be 'God's instrument for the work of the healing of the nation'. He was notable for actively practicing the paternalism which Disraeli had advocated, giving a significant portion of his wealth to the poor and campaigning for higher taxes for the rich. During his premiership new houses were built for the poor, pensions schemes were developed, women were given parity in the franchise and unemployment benefit was developed. Baldwin is a classic example of the common sense middle ground occupied by conservatives. He was not ideologically drawn to a socialist state or a *laissez faire* state. He insisted that self reliance was 'the great attribute of our people', yet nevertheless a one nation society should be developed to protect the poorest.

R. A. Butler was the intellectual mastermind of post war Conservatism. A former chancellor of the exchequer, it was in his role as the head of the Conservative Policy Unit that he detailed his ideas for 'One Nation' Conservatism. One of the items at the top of Butler's agenda was the modernisation of education. One of the most important changes he made came in the 1944 Education Act, in which he ensured secondary school was both free and mandatory up to the age of fifteen. It was Butler who made the key distinction between equality of opportunity and equality of outcome. It was because of this distinction that he ensured grammar schools were also free, as they provided the poorest in society with the opportunity to be educated at some of the very best schools in the country. It proved to be one of the most effective means of increasing social mobility, producing some of the great names of British politics during the post war period. Indeed, from Harold Wilson's ascent to the premiership until Tony Blair's, a period of over thirty years, every British Prime Minister was the product of a grammar school.

In the twenty-first century, the sensible middle ground of One Nation conservatism was pursued by Iain Duncan Smith, who had to deal with the aftermath of Labour's bloated welfare state, in which the number of workless households doubled. The former Work and Pensions Secretary likened Britain's welfare dependency culture to slavery. A passionate Christian, he believes that breaking the shackles of welfare dependency is a moral imperative for conservatives:

> As Conservatives, that is part of our Party's historic mission. Just look at Wilberforce and Shaftesbury: to put hope back where it has gone, to give people from chaotic lives security through hard work, helping families improve the quality of their own lives.[64]

His speech alludes to the Victorian mission to bring dignity and worth to the poor, who were often treated abysmally. True freedom allows individuals to realise their potential and achieve personal dignity in doing so. The overly interventionist state, advocated by socialists, prevents humans from ever realising their potential and traps them in a mindset of dependency.

Creating a more flexible labour market, incentivising work at all times and reducing the tax burden on low income earners are all important steps in helping families to break out of the malaise of welfare dependency and rewarding those who are eager to get back in to work. Helping people to move from welfare into work is fundamental to the success of a society. But, more importantly, it is a moral obligation for a government, because work is not just about making money, it is about bringing meaning and hope to people who have too often consigned themselves to unemployment, often through a lack of self worth. The belief that each of us is valuable and has something to offer brings us to one of the most fundamental ideas of conservatism, the idea of human freedom.

Chapter Four

FREEDOM UNDER LAW

True freedom requires the rule of law – Lord (Jonathan) Sacks

The General Election of 1983 loomed on the horizon. The Labour Party, under the leadership of Michael Foot, had lurched to the left, proposing a radical manifesto. The great ideological battles of the 1970s were about to reach their apogee. To which banner would the British public rally? Margaret Thatcher stood in front of an assembly of Scottish Conservatives in Perth, a small city on the banks of the River Tay. Her piercing glare swept across the audience as she declared, 'the choice facing the nation is between two totally different ways of life'. The assembled Scots listened intently. 'And what a prize we have to fight for: no less than the chance to banish from our land the dark, divisive clouds of Marxist socialism and bring together men and women from all walks of life who share a belief in freedom.' The stark dichotomy presented by Thatcher defined the politics of the 1980s.

Since that time, conservatism has had a complex relationship with the term 'freedom'. There are certainly conservatives who believe that the 1980s was characterised by an idea of freedom which was too simplistic. While it is true that freedom is central to the conservative idea of human flourishing, it is an idea of freedom that is not just qualified, but enriched, by law.

The modern liberal tradition has a different understanding of freedom. The French revolutionaries wrote in their *Declaration*, 'Liberty consists in the freedom to do everything which injures no one else'. They followed Rousseau in seeking the absolute liberation of humanity from the chains of human tradition and society. This is a mantra that has been taken up by modern liberals in Britain ever since the 1960s.

In the quest to liberate the human will, cultural norms have been relentlessly upturned; traditional institutions and social mores have been ridiculed. It is not hard to detect that the common motif behind these cultural trends is a deeply ingrained contempt of authority. While this is presented by liberals as emancipation from out of date ethics, the reality is that the poorest and the least educated have been hit hardest by the message 'do whatever you enjoy'. The conservative tradition, by contrast, has an idea of liberty which is more substantial than a simple rejection of authority; indeed it relies on us being shaped by healthy forms of legal and moral order.

Legal and moral order

Legal order and moral order are not identical. There are areas of morality that are inappropriate for legislation; equally there are areas that are appropriate for legislation which are not directly moral. Nevertheless, the two are related. Law provides a basic moral and regulatory framework within which a culture is able to develop, for good or ill.

The work of the English common lawyers such as John Fortescue and John Selden paved the way for the conservative tradition.[65] The nature of the law which they practised was inherently conservative insofar as it was built upon precedent. The judgments of the past steered the judgments of future jurists. Developing law in this fashion meant that it was tailored to the people that it was intended to serve. It offered them the ordered freedom of established English rights and customs and rejected the idea of seigniorial justice, under which barons or magnates could administer justice as they chose.

The idea that might is right was roundly rejected for one very clear reason. The key legal theorists of the English common law argued that there is a moral law operative in the universe from which our laws are derived.[66] This natural moral law was equally applicable to kings and commoners, Indians and Englishmen.

This conviction was well illustrated when Edmund Burke expressed his dismay at the treatment of Indians by the Governor-General of Bengal, Warren Hastings. Burke argued that Hastings violated the natural moral law, by flouting the innate human dignity of the Indian people. He remonstrated that 'We are all born in subjection – all born equally, high and low, governors and governed, in subjection to one great, immutable, pre-existent law'. Burke believed it self-evident that the moral law in India made the same fundamental demands upon us as the moral law in Britain.

This idea, of an objective moral law that transcends geography, culture and human conventions, seems to be something most of us believe in. There are very few people who would argue that if they landed on a remote island without laws, it would therefore be morally acceptable to murder someone – or that just because the Jim Crow laws (which enforced segregation in the Southern USA) existed, they were morally right. In other words, we intuitively sense that laws do not create our moral order, but rather they ought to reflect a moral order inherent in creation.[67] As Edmund Burke put it 'All human laws are, properly speaking, only declaratory; they may alter the mode and application, but have no power over the substance of original justice'.

For conservatives, civil law has a moral character, signposting right from wrong, even if only by implication.[68] It is tailored to the character and traditions of a people, but nevertheless resides within the bounds of the natural moral law. As Aristotle pointed out in *Nicomachean Ethics*, the form which justice takes may vary from culture to culture, but the demands of justice remain the same, irrespective of man's opinions. At a basic level then, our law ought to promote moral ends, incentivising behaviours conducive to the common good and disincentivising the most damaging behaviours. In this sense the civil law is the *sine qua non* of freedom, insofar as it protects us from the government and our fellow citizens, while securing some of the basic goods which humans require to flourish. Yet this is not the end of the story when it comes to freedom. For conservatives there is a deeper and more human account of freedom, which does not rely upon government and cannot be guaranteed by civil law.

Freedom and the moral law
For most, the necessity of legal order is obvious. The idea of radical autonomy does not just limit our freedom as individuals; it limits the freedom of those around us. If a driver chooses to disregard traffic regulations or a banker flouts financial laws, it has consequences that extend beyond themselves. There is no credible political position today

which advocates the transgression of civil law, but what we do see is a move toward a society in which the idea of a moral law is almost entirely discredited in our culture. In other words, within the bounds of civil law almost anything is deemed permissible. The idea of a substantial shared morality in our culture, in which behaviour may be legal but is nevertheless morally unacceptable, has been significantly eroded.

At face value the idea that our society would be more free if it cultivated a moral culture is counterintuitive. Surely true freedom would involve maximising our autonomy: as Frank Sinatra framed it, the ability to do things 'my way'. *Pace* Sinatra, the conservative account of freedom has taken a different view. To understand why, we need to ask what true human freedom really is.

Imagine two men, Joe and Chris. Joe is a married man with a job which he enjoys. He has two children and a voluntary role coaching teenagers at the local football club. Chris is an alcoholic who cannot commit to a relationship. He had dreams of being a soldier but lacked the commitment or character to finish his training. He has serious debt issues which have recently led to profound mental anxiety. Which of the two men is more free? Joe certainly has more self imposed obligations; indeed as a married father he has more legal obligations. Chris, on the other hand has pursued a life of extreme autonomy, he has done what he wants, when he wants, albeit within the bounds of law. But on a human level he has tethered himself to a destructive lifestyle and in doing so curtailed his own freedom. One only needs to speak to someone whose life has been destroyed by alcoholism to realise that such a lifestyle can be every bit as corrosive of human freedom as oppressive laws.

Aristotle, perhaps the greatest of the ancient Greek philosophers, argued that human nature is created for specific ends; or, to put it differently, there are specific things which are good for humans and if we pursue these things then we will flourish. This is known as teleology from the Greek word *telos* meaning 'end'.[69]

Aristotle pointed out that all creatures are created according to a design. There is, in other words, a 'functional organisation that the individuals share with other members of their species'. To be a lion means something more than just looking like a lion, because what really makes it a lion is 'its soul, the set of vital capacities, the functional organisation, in virtue of which it lives and acts'.[70] Humans, Aristotle argued, also have a design, an inherent order within them that makes them human.

It follows from this that we are not simply robots that can do as we please without biological, emotional or moral consequences. There are things that are biologically good for us and things that are biologically bad for us. When people cultivate an addiction to drugs, smoking or fatty foods, they harm their natural design and are often physically debilitated in a number of ways, meaning they are less physically free than they would otherwise be. Similarly, there are things that are morally good for us and things that are morally bad for us. If we lie or steal or cheat, we distort and corrupt our human character, which constrains our ability to form healthy relationships, develop a good character or live as a healthy and flourishing human being.

You do not need to accept everything Aristotle says to acknowledge that those who live moral lives and pursue things which enrich their mind, body and soul enjoy a more fulfilling and free existence than those who do not. Conversely, a life filled with substance abuse, broken relationships and a fixation on unhealthy pursuits, brings very real constraints to human freedom.

The fact that our nature is ordered in a certain way has implications for our understanding of politics. As Russell Kirk put it:

If you want to have order in the commonwealth, you first have to have order in the individual soul.

The idea that a culture which is conducive to healthy patterns of life will lead to a more healthy society may seem obvious, but it runs counter to the predominant assumptions of modern liberalism, which eschews any form of teleology. This is not a trivial matter, but a fundamental one, since it hinges upon what we mean by freedom.

Where liberals believe that the maximisation of choice constitutes personal freedom, conservatives believe that 'there cannot be genuine freedom unless there exists also genuine order'.[71] In other words, our freedom to be fully human is contingent upon cultivating order within our lives. It follows from this that a culture which promotes morality over vice is an important part of nourishing a healthy shared existence. Importantly, this is not about enforcing a substantive moral vision through the civil law, but making a common morality culturally normative. If we simply negate the language of morality in our culture and rely upon legislation to maintain civil order, then the worst excesses of human nature are bound to prosper.

T.S.Eliot in *The Idea of a Christian Society* expressed his concern that a culture which originally promotes itself as a neutral sphere of liberal freedom inevitably descends into the marketing of damaging moral behaviours. As he put it, many are now trapped:

> in a network of institutions from which we cannot dissociate ourselves: institutions the operation of which appears no longer neutral, but non-Christian. And as for the Christian who is not conscious of his dilemma – and he is in the majority – he is becoming more and more de-Christianised by all sorts of unconscious pressure: paganism holds all the most valuable advertising space.

Conservatives have argued that civil society is the proper forum for realising our personal freedom; again, the full demands of the moral law should not be imposed by the civil law. Nevertheless, there exists a continuum between the private and the public, the civil and the political which has been understated in liberal political theory. In the long run, a culture which promotes moral order is likely to enhance civil order, insofar as our culture shapes our lifestyles and attitudes. In promoting acceptable standards of behaviour in civil society, we also allow the government to govern with a lighter touch. The converse is also true. This is precisely why liberalism permits us ever greater moral autonomy, but simultaneously ushers in an overbearing and excessively regulatory state.

To the modern ear this may all sound rather nebulous. Yet, whatever language we use to express such ideas, their reality is hard to deny. In Britain today we can see some of the consequences of a society broadcasting the message 'do what you enjoy'. We have witnessed the proliferation of STIs, a steep rise in abortions, rocketing levels of knife crime, marital breakdown, widespread drug abuse and spiralling levels of depression. The less immediate consequences are perhaps even worse – drug abuse lines the pockets of drug dealers who further exploit communities, schools are dragged down by children who have never known discipline or stable homes, hospitals are overwhelmed by obesity and diabetes, and cities are fragmented, leading to ethnic and religious tensions.[72] All of this has been accompanied by an unprecedented rise in the number of criminal laws, workplace regulations and commissions dictating what we can or cannot say or do.

Such a social malaise limits people's opportunities. It traps them in deeply destructive patterns of behaviour, robs them of their dignity and prevents them from enjoying the type of healthy community that humans are meant to enjoy. The abdication of moral responsibility has profound consequences for our personal and political freedom, but it also has profound consequences for those around us. To take just one example, in recent years more children have been sent into care than ever before. In 2018 there were a shocking 75,420 young people in care in England, up 4% from the previous year and up by more than 25,000 children since 1994.[73] This figure equates to 90 children being taken into social care on any given day. There are of course many legitimate reasons that children go into care, but a staggering 47% of the serious case reviews involved parental substance misuse, when analysed in a 2014 government report.[74] In the light of such figures it is hard to avoid the conclusion that the liberal prioritisation of individualism is not simply harmless.

The rapid decline of moral order is hardly unprecedented in Britain. In the early eighteenth century, gin drinking and gambling became endemic in Britain. Social reformers and Christian ministers realised that the freedom to consume alcohol all day is no freedom at all. It resulted in the psychological enslavement and physical degradation of individuals, vividly depicted in Hogarth's *Gin Lane* (1751). Hogarth's friend Henry Fielding published several works, pointing out that the depravity was due to the public abandonment of morality. In reaction to the moral degradation of the nation, Methodists (led by George Whitefield and John Wesley) preached piety, holiness and personal salvation, but also worked tirelessly to provide very practical ways to help people escape from poverty, debt and addiction.

When we reflect on the root causes of social disorder and community fragmentation, the link between moral order and social order is quickly apparent. Moral order is in fact the wellspring of social order. It is the soft whisper of conscience which stops most people coming into contact with the brick wall of law. The only other viable alternative is the imposition of social order by state force which, as moral order recedes, is increasingly a necessity.

Freedom from the state

In 1958 the liberal philosopher Isaiah Berlin delivered his inaugural lecture at the University of Oxford. In the address he made the distinction which we have been looking at, between positive and negative liberty. According to Berlin, negative liberty is simply a lack of obstacles, or interference in our lives, whereas positive liberty is the process of realising our full potential.

We have already seen that conservatism consists in more than just the negative liberty of a libertarian state. Does this then mean the state should try to maximise the positive liberty of individuals by becoming heavily involved in their lives? This is certainly the socialist view. In modern liberal societies in which governments try to ensure equality of outcome, it is increasingly the prevailing liberal view. The conservative tradition has rejected this idea, opting instead for limited government and looking to civil society as the forum in which our freedoms are most likely to be realised.

To understand why this is, we must ask a more fundamental question. What is the role of government? Oliver O'Donovan defines the primary role of government as 'administering judgement according to standards of justice'.[75] In other words, a government's primary role is to prevent or respond to 'injury to the public good'. This does not mean that the government usurps the function of the judiciary, but in a broader sense it exercises sound judgement in its administration, promoting a fundamental standard of justice. This may be in actively promoting a prospective good, the absence of which would damage its citizens. We might supplement O'Donovan's definition by adding the conservative belief that, where it is possible for prospective wrongs to be remedied by civil society, they should be.

The reason that O'Donovan proposes this modest, though not minimalist, account of government is because 'not everything we do is to be determined by political judgement'. In arguing this he preserves space for civil society. To believe that everything must be resolved by politics is the road to totalitarian ideology in which '*some* abstract social design must be imposed'. By contrast, if we conceive of government as primarily exercising necessary judgement in response to wrong, then we are left with an idea of society which 'supposes that harmony is not a design conceived in a ruler's head, but a nexus of communications that exist and flourish antecedently'.[76]

Edmund Burke observed of governments, 'the greater the power, the more dangerous the abuse'. It was this perception that lay behind the checks and balances which the American founding fathers embedded within the US constitution. As Alexander Hamilton put it 'you must first enable the government to control the governed; and in the next place, oblige it to control itself'.[77]

The danger of a 'nanny' state is that it gives the government a vast amount of control, a phenomenon that is increasingly evident with the rise of digital surveillance. Moreover, the breakdown of civil society opens up new avenues for government involvement in our lives. History tells us that such power is hard to separate from the personal ambition and convictions of those who wield it.

In a nation with limited government, the state's role is to represent the moral consensus of the nation in a limited variety of areas suitable for public engagement. There is clearly a debate to be had as to what these areas are, but we might cite infrastructure, basic healthcare provision, law enforcement and defence as examples of appropriate areas for government involvement. If the reach of government activity becomes over-extended, it can radically shape a society according to its own vision; it ceases to govern and assumes an oppressive role. For conservatives, human development and edification is far more effectively achieved in our own communities, by shaping the culture that we live in through civil society.

As Tocqueville, pointed out, if we allow the government to erode the predominance of civil society, it is left virtually unopposed:

Governments therefore should not be the only active powers: associations ought, in democratic nations, to stand in lieu of those powerful private individuals whom the equality of conditions has swept away.[78]

When Adolf Hitler was granted emergency powers in 1933, the first thing he sought to do was crush the Weimar constitution's provision for the freedom of association.[79] The Romanian dictator Nicolau Ceauşescu retained power for decades by ensuring that he stifled the organic networks of civil society and placed his apparatchiks at the head of civil associations. The story has been the same the world over: from Muammar Gaddafi in Libya to Idi Amin in Uganda; Paul Biya in Cameroon to Islam Karimov in Uzbekistan; and Enver Hoxha in Albania to Gustáv Husák in Czechoslovakia. The twentieth century has been littered with authoritarians and tyrants who have sought to stifle civil association and thereby tighten their own hold on power.

Other than the excessive control the overbearing state affords governments, one of the problems with it is that individuals are denied personal responsibility for their lives. A culture of excessive regulation and micro-managing of our personal lives, risks stunting our common sense and suffocating our talents. Invariably it is the poorest who suffer.

As David Cameron pointed out in 2009, the huge expansion of government under New Labour actually led to a more unequal state, in which the poor got poorer. He noted that the number of people in severe poverty rose by 900,000 in the first decade of the twenty first century. Moreover, youth unemployment increased and social mobility stalled.[80] All of this demonstrates that high government spending doesn't automatically lead to a reduction in inequality or positive social outcomes. The contrast with a decade of Conservative policies is stark. By 2018, one million people had been lifted out of absolute poverty; employment was at its highest ever level, with youth unemployment down 50%; the number of children in workless households dropped by six hundred thousand; the poorest fifth of households took home an additional £1,000 after inflation and income inequality had fallen.[81] All of this was achieved while wrestling with the economic fallout left by the financial crash and unprecedented government spending.

Ronald Reagan spoke of 'those who would trade our freedom for the soup kitchen of the welfare state'. What he meant by this is that if we hand too much of our lives to governments then we are dispossessed of the dignity of personal responsibility, and we are also deprived of the material benefits which come with hard work and personal development. Government should never be seen as a panacea for anything that involves risk or inconvenience. The Left's habit of turning to government as the first solution for our problems may seem like an obvious option, but often government programmes are so large and indiscriminate that they end up producing a raft of unintended consequences, by incentivising the wrong behaviours.

In a trend that started with New Labour, elements of the political left have actively promoted a society of extreme individualism sustained by big government, while simultaneously lambasting conservatives for the loss of freedom that is the result of poverty. The Centre for Social Justice identified five causes of poverty: family breakdown, educational failure, worklessness, addiction and debt. It is not reduced welfare payments that are the underlying cause of protracted poverty. To believe this, is like pointing to a person dying of cancer and diagnosing the source of their problems as an inadequate dose of painkillers. One of the most pernicious causes of intergenerational poverty has been the toxic mixture of individualism and disincentives to personal responsibility. This has not been remedied, and has in some cases been encouraged, by government welfare.[82] The result has been a culture in which autonomy has been promoted at the expense of all else.

The proliferation of law
We have seen, then, that the conservative account of freedom is contingent upon legal order, and this lawful freedom allows civil society to thrive. But excessive litigation and regulation can achieve exactly the opposite effect, suffocating civil society and creating an overbearing state which stifles human creativity.

Under New Labour, the United Kingdom saw a huge rise in the number of laws, prescribing what citizens could and could not do, including over three thousand new criminal offences. Similarly, one of the most cogent criticisms of the European Union is that it spends its time creating superfluous and unenforceable laws.[83]

A recurrent motif of this book is that conservatism resists ideological extremes and seeks a sensible middle ground. In the case of law, conservatives insist that laws are vital for the regulation of a healthy society. Yet when governments seek to use these as tools to micro-manage our lives, they become unhealthy and overbearing. They stifle common sense and innovation and prevent the healthy operation of associations, which are burdened with excessive paperwork, checks and compliance with regulations.

In business, the proliferation of law can clog the arteries of a healthy market, making a disproportionate impact on small businesses which cannot afford the costs of circumnavigating endless red tape. The result is an economic ecosystem monopolised by vast corporations. Most importantly, it makes the law unintelligible to the general public and thereby undermines the rule of law. Charles Dickens satirically wrote 'the one great principle of English law is to make business for itself'. The paradox of governments creating intricate webs of laws is that it is most harmful to the poor, who are not effectively represented, or the small business owner who cannot navigate their complexity.

Between 1983 and 2009, Parliament contrived to introduce over 4,000 new criminal offences, meaning that the sheer volume of criminal laws rendered the corpus indigestible and unintelligible to the public. Niall Ferguson has dubbed this stifling level of regulation 'the rule of lawyers', arguing that is has now usurped the rule of law.

Tocqueville warned of the danger of the endless proliferation of law by governments which fill 'society with a network of small complicated rules, minute and uniform' which will subdue the populace and rob them of their 'free agency'. Even the most 'original minds and the most energetic characters cannot penetrate' the complexity of such laws. The end result is a state of dependence in which the state 'does not tyrannise' but 'stupefies a people, till each nation is reduced to nothing better than a flock of timid and industrious animals, of which the government is the shepherd.' He noted the irony of the fact that this 'administrative despotism' would likely be established by 'the sovereignty of the people'.[84]

The desire for a reduction in the complexity of the law is not new. In the sixteenth century the young Edward VI wrote 'I wish that the superfluous and tedious statutes were brought into one sum together, and made more plain and short.' In 1867 alone over 1300 statutes were repealed. In January 2013, the government introduced a 'one in, two out' approach to business regulatory red tape. The financial relief this has afforded business is estimated to be in the hundreds of millions.[85] Yet more must be done.

While legislation has a crucial function in providing the framework for public services, it is important to resist the assumption that it is the solution to all and any problems in society. Whenever greater lists emerge of what we can and cannot say or do, it is corrosive of the very sphere of our lives that teaches us to think for ourselves and grow as communities. Rather than micromanaging the lives of citizens, we must preserve space for human beings to use their common sense and moral judgement. Inevitably this will involve accepting a degree of risk at times, but accepting such risks may mitigate far greater social ills.

Left wing and liberal authoritarianism

The political left has succeeded in constructing a cluster of associations around the very word 'conservative'. To be conservative is to be right wing, and to be right wing is to be on a spectrum which culminates in fascism. Conservatism's emphasis on civil associations, its advocacy of institutional plurality, its attachment to law and the decentralisation of power, serve to make it the least amorous bedfellow imaginable to a repressive ideology such as fascism. In stark contrast to conservatism, socialism advocates state centralisation, the nationalisation of industry, the government control of markets and state enforced equality – all hallmarks of an authoritarian regime.

Tragically, the spectre of left wing totalitarianism is being resurrected by a new generation. Throughout the last decade there has been a notable rise in authoritarianism among young people, particularly from the student left. The columnist Brendan O'Neill has termed this dictatorial demographic the 'Stepford students', in reference to their unquestioning uniformity and radical political correctness. The left now dominate our universities and the results would be risible if they were not so concerning.

Major universities have introduced 'safe spaces' in which students are protected from anything controversial. At Oxford University, law lecturers were told they should issue 'trigger warnings' if they were going to touch on a potentially sensitive subject that could 'trigger' a reaction in students. The practice of 'no platforming' speakers has led to a number of high profile speakers being banned from speaking at universities simply because they do not share the same views as the far left. Even the former foreign secretary, Boris Johnson, was no platformed at King's College London.

The pervasiveness of left wing beliefs is unsurprising given that only eleven per cent of academics said they would vote Conservative in the 2015 General Election,[86] while only seven per cent said they would vote Conservative in 2017.[87]

This tide of political correctness is now touching upon every area of university life. At several major universities the sale of mainstream tabloid newspapers has been banned. Other banned items include fancy dress, the University of East Anglia going so far as to ban sombreros as they might be deemed culturally offensive. The British National Union of Students offers some of the most stunning examples of this trend. In 2017 they attempted to prohibit clapping because it is not inclusive to deaf people. The NUS has also vowed to tackle banter, remove white authors from university reading lists and destroy the vestiges of colonialism in university syllabuses.

Foremost in the firing line of the leftist students are Christian Unions, pro-life groups, pro-Israel groups and those that could be deemed patriotic or male dominated. The most striking examples being the Cambridge University Student Union voting against a motion to promote Remembrance Sunday for fear that it glorifies nationalism and war, while the president of the Southampton University Student Union endeavoured to have a mural of WW1 soldiers taken down because it solely featured white men.

So what has given rise to this new Puritanism? In order to properly understand the reactionary students we must understand that it is the fusion of extreme liberalism and old fashioned leftism.

Let us start with liberalism. Reflecting on the grievances of these students, it is hard to avoid the conclusion that in part their outrage is the product of late modern liberalism's ego-centricism, which has given rise to a distinctive culture of victimisation. In transitioning society away from a Christian moral worldview, to a society structured around human rights and equality, the state has created a culture obsessed with the individual. A generation of young people have been raised in the belief that their individual rights and feelings are paramount, with almost no broader philosophical account of the order of relations between themselves, their community and the political structures which support them. The idea that the correlate to the abundant rights of British citizens might be a duty to serve the country upon which these rights are contingent, would seem unthinkable to many young people.

Liberalism's exultation of the individual has created a world in which feelings are more important than facts. This relativisation of truth has begotten a generation detached from objectivity. They are taught that orthodox truths are just narratives conceived by hegemonic political structures. In the absence of truth, their worldview is defined by the liberation of victims from patriarchal powers. Moral reasoning has been reduced to mere feeling. Indeed, so fixated are they upon feelings that they take the feeling of offence as a personal assault, rendering the possibility for rational argument increasingly improbable. In this way secular modernism naturally degenerates into postmodernism, a process which the prophet of modernism, Friedrich Nietzsche, predicted. As a result, universities allow the naked truth to cower and conceal itself for fear of offence, in what can only be termed the institutional perpetuation of untruths.

A vocal minority of students have directed their inchoate outrage at universities for upsetting their worldview, without realising that this is precisely what universities are supposed to do. Universities at their best are a forum of free speech, in which truth and falsity are sifted out through reasonable debate. Intellectual growth cannot be achieved without challenging and changing people's comfortable assumptions. Rather than telling students this, universities have become absurdly sensitive to student criticism, and affirm these dictatorial student voices by complying with their demands.

The second part of the diagnosis is radical leftism. This aspect of the ideological menace which is gripping our universities is not novel, but it has converged with liberalism for the first time. The Marxist dialectical account of class struggle as the defining feature of history holds a deep resonance with late modern liberalism's conception of the world as power structures that need liberating from patriarchal interests; no longer are we in the throes of an economic power struggle, but in a struggle against all structures of power.

Undergraduate study coincides with an age group who yearn to define themselves as part of something much larger than themselves. Many students hope to rectify the injustices of the world, real and perceived, by becoming part of a movement that ostensibly defends the weak and oppressed. While such motives are admirable, they often result in emotion unmitigated by reason or perspective. The obvious target for left wing students, who want to lay low the rich and elevate the poor, is the West.

Hatred of the West
The meeting of extreme liberalism and radical leftism has created a strange new breed of political correctness. The egalitarianism of the left is longstanding, but it has taken from radical liberalism a hypersensitivity to cultural offence and only applies its critique to the hegemonic monopoly of white Westerners. It is deeply critical of hierarchy, but only Western hierarchy, it is deeply critical of male hegemony, but only Western male hegemony; it is horrified by violence, unless it is conducted by minority groups. While the 'Stepford students' are the first to denounce British imperial history, they are strangely quiet on the subject of the persecution of women in the Middle East; moreover, they are ominously silent on the killing of Christians in North Africa or the evils of the South American drugs trade.

Such a conspiracy of silence is not morally harmless. It is deeply damaging to the most vulnerable. The permeation of this culture into mainstream society is what gave rise to a national grooming scandal, in which thousands of young girls were sexually abused by Asian gangs in Rotherham, Rochdale, Oxford, Huddersfield and Telford, while police were too scared to confront them for fear of being branded racist.

Leftists seem to have resolved upon the consensus that criticising other cultures can easily make one seem bigoted, or intolerant, so the ostensible solution is to criticise one's own culture. It is, after all, much easier to bask in the altruism of immolating one's own nation. This position amounts to moral cowardice.

The irony in this is that the militant left enjoys a position of almost unsurpassed privilege, while denouncing the very pedestal that they sit on. Those who vehemently denounce the West are happy to study in Western institutions, use Western banks, profit from law enforcement, infrastructure and businesses funded by Western capitalism. It seemingly does not matter that by almost every index the Western world has the best living conditions and affords more rights to its subjects than any other civilisation in history. It is true that these social goods do not put the West beyond criticism, but criticism would undoubtedly be more powerful if it were qualified by an even handed acknowledgement of the tangible goods that have been attained through inestimable sacrifice over the centuries. When no such acknowledgement is made, it simply leaves the impression that ingratitude and ignorance are a powerful concoction, which never fails to beget a sense of entitlement.

Worryingly, society is at great risk of being infected by this student borne bug. The use of social media has made it very easy for the left to direct a twitter mob of fury towards anyone who expresses views with which they disagree. When you combine this hypersensitivity to speech with government legislation that extends the definition of a hate crime beyond reasonable limits, there is suddenly a very real threat to individual liberty.[88] In August 2018 Boris Johnson wrote a telegraph column in which he *defended* the right of Muslim women to wear the burka. In the article he made a joke comparing the garb to a letterbox. Such was the storm of fury provoked that the Metropolitan Police Commissioner, Cressida Dick, had to clarify whether Johnson's comments constituted a hate crime.

As we look to the future of our nation, this toxic cocktail of radical liberalism and leftism must be challenged. The suppression of free speech is a hallmark of ideological thinking, which conservatives have always opposed. This particular wave of resurgent liberalism presents a unique challenge for a generation which has been raised in an institutionally liberal environment. In his role as Minister of State for Universities, Jo Johnson delivered a speech in which he denounced the growing 'forces of censorship' in British and American Universities. As he argued in his speech, 'freedom of speech within the law must prevail in our society, with only the narrowest necessary exceptions justified by specific countervailing policies.'[89]

The lack of reasoned debate in liberalism is abetted by the phenomenon of virtue signalling. Elements of the left thrive on public displays of virtue, no matter how misplaced. There is therefore an alluring incentive to virtue signal by condemning anything which you know will ingratiate you with your social group. Whether one agrees with those that the left seeks to stifle or not, the suppression of broad debate by condemnatory statements, devoid of argument and designed simply to signal virtue, should be a cause for concern. It creates a repressive society in which negative views are not dismantled by reason, but shut down by intimidation.

Robert Ford and Philip Cowley have demonstrated that, in general, liberals are more authoritarian and reactionary than conservatives.[90] Why might this be? Perhaps it is because the narrative which is proffered by today's political left is unbelievable and misguided. We are told that humans are born free, equal and bearers of natural rights. These are metaphysical claims and therefore articles of faith. We are also told that humans are so autonomous that they can determine every aspect of their existence; even our gender becomes a function of the will and is divorced from objectivity. According to liberalism, we can create our own world in which reality is subjectively determined by the individual. In this way liberalism naturally collapses into postmodernism. Truth itself becomes a projection of the human will, not an objective reality that is ascertained by reasoned debate. In such a world the loudest voices construct the reality we live in.[91]

Moreover, the liberal narrative simply does not admit the existence of things which we intuitively know to be true, such as the existence of good and evil. There are legal behaviours and illegal behaviours, but the idea of behaviours that are legal which nevertheless corrupt and distort our humanity is a notion entirely absent in liberalism. There is a real question as to whether liberalism has adequate conceptual categories to explain the palpable evils of drug abuse, alcoholism or adultery. The liberal narrative is not, as its adherents pretend, just the default reasonable option; it is founded on an unbelievable myth.[92] As the atheist philosopher Raimond Gaita put it:

The secular philosophical tradition speaks of inalienable rights, inalienable dignity and of persons as ends in themselves. These are, I believe, ways of whistling in the dark, ways of trying to make secure to reason what reason cannot finally underwrite. Religious traditions speak of the sacredness of each human being, but I doubt that sanctity is a concept that has a secure home outside those traditions.[93]

If we compare the Christian account of humanity to the liberal account of humanity, or the Christian narrative to the liberal narrative, you might ask yourself which better reflects the ethical character of the world as you know it? When one sees tyrants seduced by power which invariably corrupts and destroys them, or when one sees the redemptive power of love and the transformative power of grace and forgiveness, we might well question which narrative offers the most comprehensive frame for reality as we experience it.

As almost every religious tradition observes, there is an ethical arithmetic operative in the world. Though it does not always deliver justice in its entirety, it speaks of an embedded moral order and, from a Christian perspective, signposts the way to a consummation of justice and judgment. Perhaps, then, this is one reason why secular liberalism is so militant. Like the Wizard of Oz, it appears to be grand and wise, but tip back the screen and the reality is much less impressive. Its ethical arguments hide behind the veil of reason, yet its advocates are unable to offer a rationale that adequately justifies their assertions. The result is the repression of any criticism directed at their beliefs.

The line at which freedom of speech is curtailed must be when opinions stray into explicit incitement to violence or unlawfulness. There is no danger in curtailing free speech at this point, because incitement to violence, in a domestic context, never involves an argument of merit; it is, by its very nature, the abandonment of reason and the resort to force. This is a point that the archetypal defender of free speech, John Stuart Mill, made when he wrote: 'even opinions lose their immunity, when the circumstances in which they are expressed are such as to constitute their expression a positive instigation of some mischievous act'. With that exception, freedom of speech must be allowed to prevail. As Mill pointed out, if we allow censorious behaviour to repress free speech, then 'we assume our own infallibility'. Public disputation is healthy and often moderates the opinions of all parties by elucidating the rationale for their positions. Through healthy disputation we allow truth to coexist with falsity. We must believe that, in the end, truth is its own best advocate and falsity its own worst accuser. As Milton put in his *Areopagita* (1644), 'Let her and Falsehood grapple; who ever knew Truth put to the worse in a free and open encounter?'

Freedom and Equality

In 2010 the Equality Act stipulated equal treatment of individuals with regard to a number of 'protected characteristics': age, disability, gender reassignment, marriage and civil partnership, race, religion or belief, sex and sexual orientation. The Equalities and Human Rights Commission (EHRC) has been given wide ranging powers to enforce equality where it is not found. It is a sad truth that some of the most pernicious attacks on freedom in modern history have been executed in the name of equality. One reason for this is that equality is a term that is malleable enough to be contorted to serve whichever ideological ends individuals want it to.

During the French Revolution, Maximilien Robespierre and his Jacobin acolytes used equality as the pretext for murdering tens of thousands of aristocrats. The idea of equality was invoked by Leon Trotsky in instigating the October Revolution and encouraging the peasantry to murder land owning families in their beds. Equality was a concept artfully wielded by Joseph Stalin during the collectivisation of agriculture in the 1920s. This policy precipitated the death of up to 75,000 Crimean Tartars as their food was transported to other areas of the USSR. Similarly, Stalin murdered up to three million Russian Kulaks on the basis of their belief in private ownership, and their relative wealth compared to the rest of the peasantry. Dozens of other examples avail themselves to a cursory historical study. We must therefore be very precise about what we mean by equality, and why we are invoking it. Equality, perhaps more than any other social value, has the ability to corrupt good intentions and beguile people into committing great evils.

When we speak of 'equality' it is important that we first refine this very nebulous concept into two distinct categories: equality of opportunity and equality of outcome. In general, equality of opportunity is a good thing.

It allows humans to fulfil their potential and is premised on a deeper conviction that there is an inherent worth in all human beings which, subject to their own choice, ought to be realised. Too often the modern left favours equality of outcome. Equality of outcome is premised on the exact inverse of the logic behind equality of opportunity. It tells us that some individuals ought to be prioritised in employment because they possess one or more 'minority' characteristics (black, disabled, female etc.). Of course, in assessing ability and the potential of a candidate to do a job or gain a place at a university, it is often fair to take past disadvantage into account on an individual basis. But to prioritise a candidate on the basis of general characteristics, such as ethnicity, without reference to the individual circumstances, deprives others of their opportunity. Whereas equality of opportunity affirms our common humanity, equality of outcome reduces humans to one aspect of their identity and then partitions us. The call for equality of outcome from the left can be split into two categories: equality of outcome economically and equality of outcome socially. The two demands are clearly not identical but they are substantially conjoined.

Let us first touch upon the argument for economic equality. As with the other areas of conservative thought that we have looked at, there is a path of common sense to be pursued, which winds its way between the ideological edifices of the extreme left and right. It is certainly true that the government has a responsibility to help the poorest in society to achieve their full potential, chiefly through education and the provision of basic social goods. But an ideological attachment to the government rectifying inequality by enforcing equality of outcome at every opportunity ultimately leads to the bloated and inefficient distributist state of the USSR, in which millions lived and died in destitution. By contrast, Conservative administrations have repeatedly made the case for a social order which offers a safety net for the destitute, while creating opportunity and incentivising hard work, thereby giving individuals the best chance to flourish, socially and economically.

The argument for social equality is subtly different. The term 'diversity' is often coupled with equality because elements of the Left argue that there is an insufficient number of minority groups in socially advantageous positions. They therefore believe that social diversity should be enforced as a facet of social equality. But the generic term 'diversity', like 'equality', is often used a proxy for rectifying any perceived injustice that the left believes exists in society. Despite diversity quotas now being pervasive in universities and businesses, the term is too often used nebulously without a precise account of what type of diversity is being achieved and why this is desirable. Moreover, it is difficult to see how the groupings that the Left chooses to construct around the idea of diversity are not dehumanising, by clustering millions of humans together under the banner of one shared characteristic.

The predominant categories of enforced diversity in workplaces are race, gender and sexual orientation. Surely such innate traits are less significant than our common humanity. Moreover, why are we choosing these categories? Are these characteristics as significant as the experiences that have impacted the trajectory of an individual's life? Presumably the selection of characteristics operates on the assumption that such innate characteristics *have necessarily* impacted each person's life opportunities. If this is the case, then why not have diversity quotas for individuals who have lost a parent, or individuals who have been victims of abuse? Statistically, these experiences are at least as significant in determining an individual's life trajectory. The simple answer is that such an assessment would be impossible to implement or verify; simply picking characteristics and assuming that they have had a negative impact on someone's life is much more convenient. One cannot help but suspect that some of the chosen categories of the left provide a convenient antithesis to what the left is hoping to tear down. The problem with manufacturing such equality of outcome is that it gives *carte blanche* to remake an organisation according to particular traits, rather than relevant skills.

More importantly, the argument for diversity on the grounds of equality of outcome has an implicit implication that is rather more sinister. To claim that an organisation needs more black people or disabled people, is to imply that there is a sufficient difference in the content of a black man's character or natural aptitudes that he needs to be given a position on the basis of his skin colour. The underlying racism of such a policy is striking. If we believe, as we should, that an individual's skin colour is utterly unrelated to their talents or their character, we would surely not think of making it a point of selection. Such thinking is itself inherently discriminatory and demeaning to the individual.

First, it is discriminatory against those whom it excludes. For example, just because someone happens to be a white male does not mean they have had an easy life or not had to overcome tribulations. The diversity of two individuals from opposite ends of the socioeconomic spectrum within one ethnic group in Britain will be at least as pronounced as the diversity between two individuals from different ethnic groups. To assert this is simply to assert that every human is an individual who has come from a different background, with different circumstances and different abilities. Indeed, one of the least privileged groups statistically, is now working class white males, who consistently perform worse than any other ethnic group in their education.[94] They are also the least likely demographic to receive further skills training as adults.[95]

Secondly, such quotas rest upon an inherently patronising logic, which presumes that black people, disabled people or women are in some sense unable to achieve parity with their white male counterparts on an equal footing. The oft quoted idea that there is unconscious bias in selection processes has been thrown into serious doubt by recent empirical findings.[96] It is undeniable that pupils from disadvantaged backgrounds have a tougher challenge in achieving educational success. The educational attainment of those from a disadvantaged background in Great Britain is two years behind those of their peers by the end of secondary school. But, if we want genuinely underprivileged individuals of all ethnicities to have the opportunity to attend university, then we cannot take the easy option of rigging the system in their favour. We must take the long road and invest in first class education in underprivileged areas, while ensuring that our institutions have fair systems of selection. If we simply rig the system to select underprivileged groups, then we are not only using a very imprecise tool to target those in need, but we are doing genuinely underprivileged individuals no favours. A significant body of academic literature indicates that recipients of university places awarded because of quotas will soon find themselves in an environment which they have not been intellectually prepared for. As a result they are set up for failure.[97]

Where there is racism in society, quotas will only accentuate differences. Creating a one size fits all policy according to an individual's race is far too clumsy a tool to counter social deprivation. In singling out ethnic minorities for special treatment, it is the left who are carving up society along racial lines and magnifying arbitrary differences between British citizens.

The best possible option in a country that truly values equality is to provide good opportunities for all, according to which individuals from all backgrounds can thrive according to their own merit. This is the only morally correct option if we hope to give all people a fair chance, irrespective of arbitrary characteristics.

Aside from the fact that the left's solution is driven by inverted prejudices, it will also end up damaging some of our most valuable institutions. This point was made clearly in 2016, by Lord Patten, the chancellor of Oxford University, who warned that if Oxford were to be forced to accept students based on quotas rather than on academic merit then standards would inevitably be eroded: 'Quotas must mean lower standards. There are better ways of addressing social inclusion at universities.'[98]

Worryingly, the obsession of the left with equality is increasingly finding expression in law, with institutions such as the Equality and Human Rights Commission making pronouncements and pursuing legal cases against individuals with the funds of the state. We might well ask who sets the agenda for such a commission. As a statutory non-department public body, its agenda is independent of the elected government. Who then dictates its parameters? The areas it currently comments on are curiously similar to those areas of public life in which liberals demand reform. A cursory review of the EHRC's literature shows that they are not a 'neutral' organisation, but hold a very distinctive liberal worldview.[99] Such a worldview bears little relation to reality and it ends up giving the government an almost limitless licence to reshape society in accordance with their definition of equality. As the independent think tank *Civitas* wrote of the EHRC:

The EHRC review details a vast range of statistical differences between social groups in Britain. However, it makes little attempt to establish what, if anything, is responsible for these differences.

Instead, when the differences appear to disadvantage some groups, it is assumed to be the result of Britain's unfairness.[100]

Unless such a commission has very tightly regulated guidelines it can easily end up using its powers and the law, to persecute any individual who opposes its worldview, thereby undermining healthy traditions and institutions. Fortunately, in the UK our courts are still independent and are able (when the law permits) to decide in favour of the individual.

As George Orwell illustrated in *Animal Farm*, equality is a slippery concept, and when the state wields equality as a tool of social control, some inevitably end up more equal than others. We should heed Tocqueville's warning that if democracies become increasingly illiberal it will not be by force, but by their own acquiescence, as people look to the state for all their needs. It is the 'principle of equality' that has 'prepared men for these things [the increased powers of the state]; it has predisposed men to endure them and often to look on them as benefits'.

Chapter Five

COMMUNITY

One can acquire everything in solitude except character – Stendhal

I have identified socialism and liberalism as two enduring political opponents of conservatism. The former purports to prioritise society but does so in a way which stifles the freedom of civil society; the latter gives absolute precedence to individuals and their rights. Conservatism is a middle road between these positions. It acknowledges that without individuals there can be no community, and yet maintains that communities provide the necessary context for the flourishing of the individual.

The power of community

On December 1st 1955, an African American seamstress called Rosa Parks stepped onto a bus and America was never the same again. Why? Because the irrepressible power of community solidarity refused to accept the injustice she suffered. In the 1950s, the Jim Crow Laws had given legal justification for discrimination against blacks, institutionalising deep racial injustices. Rosa Parks' offence was refusing to move from her seat for a white man, when she was asked to by James F. Blake, the white bus driver. She was subsequently arrested and made to pay a fine.

Under the leadership of E. D. Nixon and Martin Luther King Jr., black people across Montgomery boycotted the bus services. The economic impact was immediate and felt sorely by the public transport services. As the strike went on, the black community began to innovate and adapt, by sharing lifts, lowering the price of taxis and holding public meetings in churches. The Christian community leaders united the black community around the Christian belief that all humans are of equal and of inestimable worth in God's eyes, meaning that segregation premised on racial inferiority was inherently unjust. The movement soon bred local clubs and associations, providing support to each other and raising money for those in need. The boycott continued for over a year. In late December 1956, victory was won. Both the federal district court and the United States Supreme Court ruled that segregation on public bus services was illegal. The shockwaves of the boycott were felt across America, shaking the system and highlighting the injustices that black people continued to suffer.

The story illustrates the features of community that we will look at in this chapter. It shows us the latent potential of a community to be a force for good in the world, applying pressure until laws conform to the demands of justice. The story highlights how associations can produce ideas and strengthen relationships, and it illustrates the centrality of moral values to the life of a community. Conversely, the deep segregation of the community in Montgomery is a reminder of how discordant a community can become if we allow injustice to flourish and neglect our fellow citizens.

In this chapter we will look at the importance of community in conservative thought. We will begin by asking why community matters before questioning what changes in the modern world mean for its future.

Why community matters

John Donne famously wrote that 'no man is an island'. We are changed, developed and affected by the behaviour and beliefs of those around us. Conservatism sees community as a moral enterprise for this reason. It is an enterprise undertaken by neighbours, friends and family and it is composed of human relationships between people who know each other and are therefore best placed to help each other. The converse side to this fact is that, if we do not facilitate the growth of healthy communities, the effect on individuals can be disastrous.

This insight was recognised by George W. Bush when he founded the White House Office of Faith-Based and Community Initiatives, in the conviction that federal funds are best administered by local agencies, particularly religious institutions which are often deeply engaged with caring for the poor and the broken. When we go abroad we seek local knowledge. Similarly, when we want to find solutions to local issues it is often local communities who are best placed to provide them. Our communities are our networks of support, commerce and friendship.

Russell Kirk, perhaps the greatest American conservative intellectual of the twentieth century, wrote that 'conservatives uphold voluntary community, quite as they oppose involuntary collectivism'. What Kirk realised, as Burke and Tocqueville realised before him, is that radical individualism and big government are two sides of the same coin. If either of them is over-emphasised they soon become mutually reinforcing; it is for this reason that modern liberalism and socialism increasingly seem hard to distinguish from each other. Autonomous citizens look to the state alone for their security, and the state gains ever more power by setting itself up as the sole guarantor of a citizen's rights. This symbiotic relationship between individualism and the big state naturally erodes community and personal responsibility.

The attrition of community in Britain is bad news for many reasons, but one of the most important reasons is that civil society is the area of public life in which we are free to pursue our most deeply felt human desires, which cannot be satisfied by the state. Tocqueville's *Democracy in America* contains a sobering warning in its final pages. He speaks of a 'species of oppression by which democratic nations are menaced' which does not consist in 'despotism and tyranny', but something 'more extensive and more mild' which would 'degrade men without tormenting them'.

In this remarkable passage he foresees 'an innumerable multitude of men, all equal and alike, incessantly endeavouring to procure the petty and paltry pleasures with which they glut their lives. Each of them, living apart, as a stranger to the fate of all the rest'. Under such circumstances, Tocqueville warns, a man would see his fellow citizens but 'not feel them; he exists only in himself and for himself alone', even if he retained his friends he would have 'lost his country'.

Tocqueville prophesied that the end result of such egalitarianism would be 'an immense and tutelary power' which stands over the citizens and 'takes upon itself alone to secure their gratifications and to watch over their fate… It would be like the authority of a parent,' but unlike a parent it seeks to 'keep them in perpetual childhood'. This big government will gradually involve itself in all the affairs of men, 'for their happiness such a government willingly labours, but it chooses to be the sole agent and only arbiter of that happiness; it provides for security, foresees and supplies their necessities, facilitates their pleasures, manages their principle concerns, directs their industry... what remains, but to spare them all the care of thinking and all the trouble of living?'.[101]

The rise of the 'nanny' state has emerged in tandem with a relentless rights discourse which focuses on what is ostensibly owed to individuals. The liberal conception of the individual as a solitary rights bearer not only gives credence to large government but it perpetuates its own conception of the individual; liberalism has sold us the flattering lie that we are not dependent upon others. Big government sustains this mirage by providing all our basic securities. Selbourne reminds us that the individual cannot be thought of as 'a mere bundle of rights which may be asserted against the civic order of which he is a member'.[102] Not only will it lead to a grave extension of government and unsustainable financial burdens, but it will prove disastrous for the individual.

We will never be fulfilled or happy if our primary relationship is with the government. Government might be able to cater to some of our material needs, but it will never provide the authentic community which addresses our deepest emotional and spiritual needs. David Cameron was absolutely right to suggest that as the state has grown it has taken away from people 'more and more things that they should and could be doing for themselves, their families and their neighbours'. The end result has been a change in 'the character of our society – and indeed the character of some people themselves, as actors in society'.

At the heart of this change is a loss of community. Cameron pointed out that 'there is less expectation to take responsibility, to work, to stand by the mother of your child, to achieve, to engage with your community, to keep your neighbourhood clean, to respect other people and their property, to use your own discretion and judgement'.[103] If we do not recognise this observation in our political discourse, then we risk believing that the more hypothetical rights a person is given by their government, the happier they will be. As we will see, the historical result of this mistake has been the creation of societies which may have suited hypothetical citizens, but were disastrous for real, flesh and blood human beings. Equally damaging to community, is the extreme consumerism that has become a central part of our culture. In the absence of a community orientated culture, we have come to believe that material wealth is the only path to human happiness.

It is a fascinating development in the modern world that, in spite of unprecedented levels of material wealth and increased consumer choice, levels of happiness are not notably improving; indeed the opposite seems to be true. In his book *Happiness: Lessons From A New Science*, the British economist Lord (Richard) Layard has shown that there seems to have been no increase in our levels of happiness over the last fifty years, in spite of our average level of wealth doubling. First world countries now have much higher levels of depression and alcoholism than they did half a century ago.[104] Wealth is clearly a social good; but the evidence seems to suggest that if we pursue wealth at the expense of all else, we will not necessarily be happier. Everyone, from political theorists to workplace consultants and personal gurus, is now asking questions which were commonplace in Plato's Academy during the fourth century BC; most fundamentally, what is happiness?

In spite of our endless material acquisitions, rates of happiness are not increasing, as materialism ultimately lacks the resources to honour the cheque it offers. If our quest is to foster a culture that satisfies our species' most deeply held needs, it is hard to avoid the conclusion that we have lost our way. In a 2016 Red Cross survey, 32% of 16-24 year olds said they often or always feel lonely. These findings are echoed in a 2018 report in which 65% of the same demographics said they feel lonely at least some of the time. The figure is not much better for the broader population, with nearly half of those surveyed feeling lonely some of the time.[105]

In 2018 the British government appointed a minister for loneliness, due to the 'epidemic' levels of isolation afflicting people. A 2017 report found that nine million people often or always feel lonely, while 3 out of 4 GPs say they see between 1 and 5 people a day who come in because they are lonely. One in ten GPs sees 6-10 such patients daily, while loneliness costs employers £2.5 billion per year![106] In case one was tempted to believe this was a peculiarly British issue, the situation is no better in many other advanced Western economies; for example, a staggering third of US citizens identified as lonely.

These figures might prove unsurprising when we reflect on a recent NatCen Social Research survey which found that only a quarter of British people are very positive about their community, with only around half of British adults saying they have a strong sense of community.[107]

All of these results reflect the fact that humans are social by nature and our thirst for intimacy and meaningful relationships are not being met. There is a profound aspiration at the heart of the human condition, which consists in the desire to be known and valued. Liberalism has consistently prioritised connectivity over real personal connection and image over intimacy; it is unsurprising that the end result has been a generation which is increasingly isolated.[108]

Perhaps the most worrying aspect of this decline of community is the risk that it will impede the development of the basic human traits which democracy requires.

Community and Character

From a very young age the mundane interactions of our everyday lives teach us civic virtue. Aside from their formal education, schoolchildren are tacitly educated by their interactions in the playground and on the sports field. They learn what their peers find funny, hurtful, entertaining and admirable. This education continues into our adult lives: in the university, the workplace, the pub and so forth. In these forums, we are inculcated with a lesson that is basic to the function of a civilised society: our behaviour has an effect on others, just as the behaviour of others has an effect upon us.

In these public forums we are brought into contact with a profusion of people whose eccentricities and faults we are obliged to tolerate and even come to appreciate. The antidote for intolerance is affection and affection is bred by familiarity. This is illustrated powerfully in the film *American History X*, in which the protagonist, Derek Vinyard, is a Neo Nazi gang leader who is sentenced to prison for the manslaughter of an African-American. While in prison he is put in charge of the prison laundry alongside an African-American man called Lamont. They develop a friendship around the common interest of basketball and as a result his caricature of black men is broken down and he comes to see Lamont as a human being. His familiarisation with 'the other' through a shared interest results in him developing a friendship and acts as the catalyst for the transformation of his character. Community is central to the formation of human character. At its best, it brings our jagged edges into contact with those of others. Gradually we are smoothed and rounded.

One of the most important features of communities which arises from the accident of geography is that they force us to encounter individuals who may have very different backgrounds to us. Engagements with such people encourage broad mindedness, the exchange of ideas and tolerance. Concerns have been raised by psychologists as to whether this humanising process is still taking place among young people. Sue Palmer, a child psychologist, has shown that the use of media as a replacement for normal childhood interactions is forming a generation of young people who find socialising far more difficult and whose natural creativity and imagination have been greatly stifled. Worryingly, she also points out that there is a large body of data indicating that empathy is also stifled. This should be a cause of concern for democracies and healthy societies, which run on the fuel of human empathy.

Empathy for those around us is at the heart of authentic community. Interestingly, it is a virtue which most perceive to be lacking in conservatives. Numerous studies have shown that conservatives are perceived to be less generous and empathetic than liberals. Arthur C. Brooks, an American social scientist, looked extensively at the empirical data regarding which demographic groups are the most charitable in American public life. Confounding his expectations, it wasn't liberals, but conservatives who gave the most to charity. He writes:

> Before I started the research... I assumed that those people most concerned and vocal about economic inequality would be the *most* likely to give to charity. But I was wrong. Instead, I found a large amount of data all pointing in the same direction: For many people, the desire to donate other people's money displaces the desire to give one's own. People who favour government income redistribution are significantly less likely to behave charitably than those who do not.[109]

Conservatives know that if there is going to be a change in the world, then they will have to work for it and pay for it themselves.[110] The most striking finding was the size of the gap between liberal and conservative benevolence; conservatives gave thirty per cent more in charitable donations than their liberal peers.

The fact that this finding defies people's expectations is probably a testament to how strongly conservatives have focused on trumpeting the free market and limited government at the expense of the other half of the conservative equation: community, human empathy and the charity that flows from this.

Brooks also observed that such engagement in civil society through the giving of time and money did not just benefit society; it shaped the individual. This reinforces what we intuitively know from our experience which is that our community shapes our character. Those who contribute to their community have a strong positive correlation to other socially desirable traits, such as tolerance, sympathy, politeness and honesty. Being civically engaged is also associated with lower levels of racism, prejudice and bigotry.[111]

If our society is indeed struggling with an epidemic of loneliness, then community is the antidote. There are three foundational social institutions which give us a good starting point if we hope to counter the excesses of modern individualism: marriage, the family and the church.

Marriage and the Family

Edmund Burke believed that 'The Christian religion, by confining marriage to pairs, and rendering the relation indissoluble, has by these two things done more toward the peace, happiness, settlement, and civilization of the world, than by any other part in this whole scheme of divine wisdom.'[112] We have heard of Edmund Burke's little platoons of community association, but perhaps the most fundamental unit of association for conservative tradition is the relation between man and wife. As Pope Francis put it:

> This complementarity is the foundation of marriage and the family, which is the first school where we learn to appreciate our gifts and those of others, and where we begin to learn the art of living together. For most of us, the family constitutes the principal environment in

which we begin to 'breath' values and ideals, as well as to realize our potential for virtue and charity.

When we are born, a natural affection for our parents, siblings and even more remote relations, is ingrained in our mind. There are clearly good biological reasons for this phenomenon, though it would be wrong to reduce such affection to evolutionary utility. The importance of our parents and the immediate family unit remains undiminished in our modern societies. We learn from a very young age that love involves discipline, we learn that having privileges also entails taking on responsibilities, and we learn that our egotistical nature must be tempered if we are to exist harmoniously with our peers. In the context of our family units we have our most basic questions about the world answered for us by those who have the patience to bear their banality.

A huge increase in single parenthood has emerged since the late 1960s. Between 1971 and 1991 the number of lone parent families doubled. From 1970 to 2011 the number of lone parent families in Great Britain has tripled, the figure rising to around 25 per cent in the UK as a whole and 29 per cent in England and Wales. Most strikingly, the number of single mothers who have never married has risen by a factor of ten during this period.[113] By just about any social metric these figures are not good news.

There has been a tragic social and economic cost to the liberalisation of traditional values around marriage in the 1960s. The breakdown of family life is consistently cited as one of the chief causes of crime and social disorder. As Dr Patrick Fagan has pointed out, over the past decades there has been a direct correlation between the rise in family breakdown and the rise in community crime.[114] Fagan points out that, historically, crime cannot easily be linked to the deprivation of material wealth. When the US economy experienced a sustained period of economic growth between 1905 and 1933 America's crime rate rose, yet it dropped during the Great Depression. He cites the example of the Chinese population of San Francisco in the mid 1960s, who were economically the poorest of any ethnic group in the area yet had the lowest levels of crime.

In short, there is a far more clear and consistent link between family breakdown and crime, than there is between material wealth and crime.

As Fagan argues, this has broader consequences for the community that often cause the perpetuation of the cycle:

> The empirical evidence shows that too many young men and women from broken families tend to have a much weaker sense of connection with their neighbourhood and are prone to exploit its members… this contributes to a loss of a sense of community and to the disintegration of neighbourhoods into social chaos and violent crime.[115]

Beyond crime, there has been an enormous economic cost of family breakdown. Statistically, lone parents households are far more likely to be unemployed, 50 per cent compared to under ten per cent of households headed by a couple.[116] Educational prospects are also significantly diminished. The social disorder this has caused goes hand in hand with a vast expansion of the welfare state. As the journalist David Goodhart acknowledged, 'A more individualistic society has led to a bigger, more intrusive state as the family and, more intangibly, the community have weakened.'[117] The annual cost of family breakdown in the UK is £48 billion, which covers a vast array of subsidies from child tax credits to income support.[118]

The collapse of a family is clearly tragic for all involved and there are often many complicating factors. Yet, the outcome of a culture which has less esteem for traditional marriage is a significant proportion of young people growing up without the stabilising influence of two parents in their lives. This has repeatedly been shown to result in diminished life outcomes as well as an array of negative psychological consequences.[119] Unfortunately, the West's relentless emphasis on personal autonomy has too often led to the abdication of responsibility. The consequences are, in large part, borne by the next generation.

A conservative response to family breakdown should seek to defend marriage from its detractors who often seem to seize upon individual autonomy with little thought for its wider effects. Importantly, a compassionate response to those who have suffered traumatic marriages is perhaps the best way to allay the reservations of those who denigrate the very notion of a lifelong commitment. Where shame has been weaponised in the past to scorn those who have suffered the tragedy of an abusive relationship, we must, as a society, learn hard lessons. Pharisaic attitudes are a fuel for the opponents of marriage. Rather than a culture of shame for those who do not choose marriage, we should promote marriage on its own virtues.

David Cameron's Conservative government sought to incentivise marriage in law, which was seen by most conservatives as a welcome affirmation of the government's support for an elementary social institution. Irrespective of the financial or legal incentives, conservatives ought to champion marriage for marriage's sake – because study after study has returned the verdict that, in spite of the cost and compromise, marriage remains one of the surest paths to happiness for the individual and their community. [120]

Church

In Christian theology the Church is the ultimate paradigm of community.[121] It refers to the corporate body of believers, who enjoy a relationship of love and generosity, bound together by their shared faith, in spite of their social, ethnic or political differences.[122] Sadly this has clearly not always been the reality of the institutional Church!

Saint Augustine spoke of two cities, one heavenly and one earthly, the former being the corporate body of true believers past and present, the latter being the world, including the fallible institutional church. While the Church of England is not the heavenly city, it has nevertheless endeavoured to realise the type of community envisaged by the early church, who put aside their differences in the knowledge that they were one in Christ. In doing so it has shaped the nature of community in the British Isles for well over a millennium. Moreover, it has furnished the British people with a common morality which has been the oxygen of their shared national life.

The Church parish in England dates back to the seventh century and was formally established throughout England by the twelfth century. While parishes are administrative areas, they are also communities in which old and young, rich and poor, gather in the same place of worship and share the same communion bread. Throughout the colourful tapestry of English history the parish has provided an unbroken thread of continuity; civil war, famine, plague, rebellion, bombing, new philosophies and ancient enmities have all taken place to the ambient rhythms of the liturgical calendar, daily worship and civil administration. Not only has the church facilitated English community for centuries, but it was so integrated into English society that it provided the original prototype for many of our modern social institutions.

The parish vestry, a committee composed of ratepayers in the church community, emerged from the parochial administration of medieval towns and was responsible for administrating the parish in both ecclesial and secular matters. One of the remarkable things about these bodies is that they were not appointed by an office of state, nor were they paid by the government – they were organic entities that arose from the local community and, as such, were deeply invested in their community. Indeed, the precursor to the parish vestry can be traced all the way back to the community gatherings (known as moots) in Saxon Britain. Parish vestries instigated the common law in their region by appointing constables, clerks and other officials. They took care of the poor and administered the poor laws, they ensured the safety of the people and they cared for veteran sailors and soldiers. They also took care of the deeply practical needs of the community, by installing and maintaining community infrastructure.

This system clearly had its faults. It was undemocratic and tended to encourage a small number of individuals to hold the office in perpetuity. But for hundreds of years it was an effective way of individuals gathering together and investing in their communities. As deeply social creatures, whose deepest needs are only met by relationships, the challenge for twenty-first century humans is to facilitate engagement in our modern communities as the traditional parish once did. The prospects for us doing so are not as bleak as one might initially think. The traditional parish vestry may have been usurped in many of its functions by the modern state, but there still remain ample opportunities for those who wish to make a meaningful contribution to their local community, not least through parish councils which still retain many of their traditional responsibilities.

In 1894 the Local Government Act transferred the civil responsibilities from the church vestry to civil parish councils. Today civil parish councils provide the first tier of government across much of the country, mostly in rural areas serving around 16 million people. Their main responsibilities are 'representing the local community, delivering local services and improving quality of life and community wellbeing.'[123] Practically, this means they hold a variety of responsibilities in the local community, ranging from those connected with sports facilities, parks and burial grounds to festivals, crime reduction and street cleaning. Rather than such powers diminishing, there has in recent years been a drive towards more local, devolved government, in the belief that nobody knows the local needs of communities as well as they do themselves.

While the formal administration of community matters is no longer in the province of the Church of England, the reality is that the church and other faith based institutions are still on the front line of providing for the deepest human needs in our society, both spiritually and practically. The Salvation Army, Tearfund, Christians Against Poverty and Christian Aid are just a few examples of religious charities which annually invest millions of pounds and hours helping the poorest and most vulnerable in our society.

Faith speaks to a special need in humanity which extends beyond our material concerns. If you speak to anyone who works with the homeless you will soon realise that the heart of the human challenge is the challenge of the human heart. More often than not their needs are not simply material. Faith based communities provide a family of people who genuinely care about individuals and are willing to sacrifice their time and energy to establish relationships with them. This need for authentic relationships is common to all humans and is met by faith based communities. The strong communal aspect of religion may be part of the reason that repeated studies have shown the correlation between religion and human happiness.[124]

Beyond charity, the traditional parish, with the place of worship at its heart, offers us an effective blueprint for grassroots community association which other institutions can learn from: community sport, interest based associations, schools, co-operatives, small businesses and other religious institutions. All of these remain viable ways of forging friendships, improving our common life and bringing our communities closer together.

The breakdown of community

The Conservative MP Dominic Grieve has written 'I receive several letters a week from constituents telling me that they can no longer identify with the country that they are living in.'[125] Grieve relates how both young and old constituents say they have lost their emotional connection to Britain, 'It's like the breakdown of a personal relationship.'[126] We have already seen the necessity of the first person plural 'we' in cultivating nationhood. It is little surprise that, when citizens see their recognisable community dissolving, they feel a sense of grief and personal loss.

For Grieve, a significant amount of responsibility for this social breakdown lies with the political left which, he argues, has systematically sought to destroy the symbolic and cultural heritage of Britain over a long period of time.[127] Perhaps the most damaging 'weapon' of the left, has been 'the imperative need to adapt Britishness to diversity by multiculturalism'.[128] Indeed, Tony Blair's adviser Andrew Neather famously reported that New Labour actively pursued a policy of open doors immigration in order to undermine the Conservative party. This was done by repealing the primary purpose rule (which required spouses from overseas seeking UK residence rights to provide evidence that the purpose of the marriage was not to obtain residence), introducing a steep increase in work permit quotas and study visas while opening the door to EU immigration.

The fact that people want to come to Britain and share in our national life is something of which British people should be proud. In rebuking the damaging doctrine of multiculturalism, we must never rail against multi-ethnicism. Those who want to contribute to our country and take part in our national life should be welcomed with open arms, irrespective of ethnicity. Historically, the presence of immigrants has enriched our culture in innumerable ways. Nevertheless, there is a practical case to be made to ensure that immigration is on a scale which maximises the chances of integration into society. Today, one in four working age people in England are foreign born; this is amplified by the high density of these populations around urban centres.[129] In too many cases, Grieve argues, this has resulted in the reinforcement and legitimatisation of deep differences between British culture and those of immigrants. The result is that many second or third generation immigrants are more alienated from British society than their parents.

Sadly, the latest analysis backs Grieve up. In 2016 Dame Louise Casey led a House of Lords Select Committee enquiry. She often found 'cultural and religious practices in communities that are not only holding some of our citizens back but run contrary to British values and sometimes our laws. Time and time again I found it was women and children who were the targets of these regressive practices.' While she notes that 'the divergence of attitudes among some Muslims in Britain from the general population is concerning', she also notes that there are a number of ways in which this can be tackled, including youth schemes which integrate those of other communities.

It is not just mass immigration which has led to the disintegration of British public life. The way we conduct our politics has much to answer for. In recent years we have seen the Balkanisation of political opinion among the general public, in part fuelled by data analytics which reinforce our political preferences on social media. The need to make messages pithy and conform to the size of a tweet is too often at the expense of a balanced picture.

If a political culture is to remain healthy and vibrant, it cannot descend into a shouting match between two diametrically opposed parties; there has to be some degree of understanding and empathy. The animosity of political discourse now means that the underlying empathy, which should be the platform for political debate, has evaporated. This is accentuated by the decline in civic participation that we have been looking at.

So what can conservatives recommend in order to arrest the breakdown of British national life?

The common good
The high tide of liberal philosophy was marked in John Rawls' seminal work *A Theory of Justice* (1971), which sought to create a society in which individuals were free to pursue their own private ends. His philosophy emerges from a contractarian tradition which rejects moral realism as the foundation of our shared public life in favour of a contractual agreement between parties. Yet, nearly half a century on from this work, figures on the left and the right of the political spectrum have come to lament the idea of a society in which individuals simply seek

the fulfilment of their personal desires. More fundamentally, thinkers such as Alasdair MacIntyre denounce the very possibility of living a life of free agency. Following the philosopher Ludwig Wittgenstein, he makes the case that we are *always* conditioned by our traditions and community narratives. The idea of choosing a personal narrative in a vacuum of belief is a mirage.

In the face of modern liberalism, Aristotelian thought has been revived in political theory over the last fifty years. Non-conservative thinkers, such as Alasdair MacIntyre, have identified that human flourishing is intimately bound up with living a life of virtue within communities that share these values. As he puts it in *After Virtue*:

> The best type of human life, that in which the tradition of the virtues is most adequately embodied, is lived by those engaged in constructing and sustaining forms of community directed towards the shared achievement of those common goods without which the ultimate human good cannot be achieved. Liberal societies are characteristically committed to denying any place for a determinative conception of the human good in their public discourse, let alone allowing that their common life should be grounded in such a conception.[130]

MacIntyre is in effect saying that we have taken a wrong turn. Jettisoning a more substantial understanding of who we are as a community has caused us to lose a shared conception of the common good.

In practical terms then, what does a return to a society with a commonly held belief in the common good actually look like? Conservatives are realists and are not seeking to create a society in which individuals are *required* to be virtuous beyond the basic regulatory moral framework of the law, but rather they seek to emphasise the fact that when virtue is culturally normative it is beneficial for everyone. There are some very practical steps that we can take to ensure that notions of the good are indeed commonly held and centred upon shared values, so that we do not exist in 'balkanised' communities.

First, the introduction of civics classes into school curriculums would provide a much needed emphasis on the privileges of citizenship. In nations such as France and America, civics classes are routine. In Japan the development of character with a strong focus on civic mindedness and collective responsibility is an integral part of the education system.[131]

Given that a substantial part of a young person's life is spent in the education system it is important that schools do not see their role as simply teaching, but rather they should feel empowered to impart a more holistic education in which they nurture values of responsibility, citizenship and good character. Such virtues are likely to reap social dividends when they leave education. The curriculum should also make students aware of their nation's narrative, warts and all. When one reflects on the rights, opportunities, healthcare and heritage that British citizens have been gifted, they are very often taken for granted. A logical connection must be drawn between these things and the endeavours that secure them. Unsurprisingly, education is an integral part of developing a healthy mindset in the next generation.

Secondly, there is nothing reactionary about the desire to insist on the need for greater efforts toward the integration of immigrant communities into British society. People who have a love for Britain and want to contribute to its national life are critical to the vitality of the nation, but if we are to integrate immigrants effectively then we must do more to welcome them into our society, so that our culture is not seen as impenetrable to outsiders. In a world of competing ideologies we must be clear that being British has nothing to do with ethnicity and everything to do with a set of shared values. We must equally insist that efforts to integrate immigrants are bilateral. Multiculturalism was a damaging doctrine in this respect. Those who come to Britain must do so because they want to adopt Britain as their home and contribute to its national life, rather than create a microcosm of their native land in Britain.

Thirdly, the restoration of British community is not only contingent upon the restoration of identity, but pride in that identity. As Dean Acheson, the former United States Secretary of State, famously put it, 'Great Britain has lost an Empire and not yet found a role'. As a society, Great Britain needs to discover an identity which captures the public imagination and draws people to its cause. More than any other nation on earth, Great Britain has gifted the world with a vast array of political values, scientific advancements and artistic achievements;

from parliamentary democracy to Newtonian physics, the common law to the English language, and Shakespeare to the internet. Britain holds more Nobel Prizes than any nation on earth, other than the USA. If Trinity College, Cambridge were a country, it would rank fifth in the number of Nobel Prizes, with more than Sweden. When one reflects on Britain's achievements, the most shocking thing is how reticent British citizens are to feel any pride in their nation. A YouGov poll in 2018 found that 55 per cent of young people in England did not feel proud to be English.[132] This is something that must change if we are to enjoy a common life as a nation.

A healthy pride in our shared achievements has a magnetism which draws people to its cause, aiding integration and social participation. A sense of cultural shame and self loathing achieves exactly the opposite; it feeds fuel to our enemies and creates a divisive multiculturalism in which no one wants to share in the shame of the nation.

Honesty about our past mistakes is healthy, but it must be dealt with an even-handed acknowledgement of the great good our nation has accomplished. Britain has pushed the bounds of medicine and technology, stymied the global slave trade, halted the march of European tyrants and promulgated the rule of law. Britain's island story is rich and complex, and there is much to be proud of. The Left too often dismiss three hundred years of civilization as 'colonialism'. To do so is laziness and an injustice to the good that was achieved at great cost. If we are to arrest community fragmentation then we must rekindle a pride in our heritage and invest time, energy and initiative in promoting it.

Fourthly, we must continue to encourage the decentralisation of responsibility to local communities, while fostering a culture of voluntarism. David Cameron's *Big Society* initiative had many laudable aspirations, some of which were carried through to fulfilment. Key to the success of his ambition was ensuring that, wherever possible, central government supports local communities in taking charge of their own decisions, rather than assuming this role for itself. In order for charities, social enterprise and individuals to make the changes that they wish to see in their communities, they often require financial aid, volunteers and information. Government can play a role here by cutting red tape and also by providing grants and initiatives to aid social enterprise, an approach pioneered by *Big Society Capital*. However, government will never be able to mandate the *Big Society*; the most it can do is empower others.

A number of commentators deemed the *Big Society* initiative to be a failure, noting that many met it with apathy or bemusement. This reflects the fact that any government's aspiration to encourage community engagement will be impotent if it is not culturally normative to do so. This is why, when all is said and done, a revival of community can only be achieved by taking the long hard road of transforming attitudes. It is one reason why an educational emphasis on duty is just as important as an education in rights.

There is no reason that an advanced economy should not have a strong culture of civic engagement; in fact, the good news is that Anglophone countries account for five of the top eight nations for charitable giving over the last five years (USA, Australia, New Zealand, Canada and the UK). Interestingly, the percentage of British people who volunteer time (31%) is significantly lower than those who donate money (70%).[133] Encouraging a culture of community engagement is achievable, but, like all cultural values, it must be nurtured. We should not be surprised if this takes generations rather than a few short years. This cultural shift is not the work of any one administration; it must be pioneered by private citizens.

Finally, we must have the empathy to see perspectives other than our own. I have repeatedly stressed that conservatism is a moral and practical philosophy, not a rigid ideology. This means that we should be willing to come out of our trenches and seek common ground with those of other political persuasions. We may not always agree with them, but empathy for their perspective is at the heart of a healthy society. Humility should be a defining virtue of conservatism, due to our belief in human limitation. This means that we should never assume we have all the answers. We may well be enriched by seeing the world through the eyes of another. The benefit of this approach is that it paves the way for mutual dialogue. Conservatives must trust that such dialogue will, in the end, be beneficial.

Chapter Six

TRADITION AND CULTURE

The state ought not to be considered as nothing better than a partnership agreement...as the ends of such a partnership cannot be obtained in many generations, it becomes a partnership not only between those who are living, but between those who are living, those who are dead, and those who are to be born – Edmund Burke

It does not seem to be an overstatement to say that in the modern world 'tradition' has become a dirty word. As far back as 1911, D.H. Lawrence wrote that 'it is a fine thing... not to be dependent on tradition and second-hand ideals'.[134] In the twenty-first century, the liberal movement has succeeded in building an association between just about anything liberalism commends and the word 'progressive'. Needless to say, not everyone would agree that the world being ushered in by liberalism can be described as progress. In their depiction of themselves as pioneering progressives, there is an implicit contrast with the fusty conservative, clinging on to outmoded rituals and redundant moral values.

Do liberals have a point? Are there not areas of our public life which people have clung to purely because they are sanctified by their antiquity? The answer is surely yes.

Whatever the virtues of the Victorian and Edwardian eras, they also had failings. Women were treated as second class citizens, the poor and destitute had limited protection from the predations of criminals, and sexual and domestic abuses were closeted. It is morally obvious that there have been necessary reforms to our society and sometimes these reforms were opposed by reactionary groups of all political loyalties.

Where liberals are mistaken, however, is in the belief that the perpetuation of such injustices is somehow the cornerstone of conservatism. Indeed, it was conservatives who pioneered many of the

109

social changes that brought an end to social injustices. The key point is that a general proclivity for adhering to tradition does not preclude the acceptance of necessary change. Indeed, rather than tradition hindering the moral progress of society, conservatives believe that tradition helps to morally orientate us towards the right course of action to ensure the same mistakes are not repeated.

Why tradition matters

Imagine a scientist who announces that he is going to discard all of the discoveries and mathematical formulas of the past two thousand years and simply start again, in search of one grand scientific theory. He would surely be thought mad. Even Sir Isaac Newton famously wrote (in a letter to his fellow scientist Robert Hooke in 1675) that he stood on the shoulders of giants. This, then, is the basic conviction of conservatism: the social body is replete with the hard won lessons of the past. It is, in part, the lessons of the past that should guide and direct us as we look to the future.

Edmund Burke said that his idea of a true statesman was someone who had a 'disposition to preserve with an ability to improve'. The two are not contrary but conjoined. The Catholic theologian James F. Keenan makes the point that if we move beyond a superficial understanding of tradition, then it is 'progressive, developing, and constantly calling us to receive it, enrich it, and humanize it'.[135]

When you reflect on what tradition is in its broadest sense, it is fundamental to the continued existence of our species. Language is tradition. It is the accumulated body of idiom and grammar that has developed through tried usage over millennia. Other traditions include such things as our meal times, our shared festivals, sports and songs, our understanding of etiquette and our habituated social norms. The whole unseen structure of our social existence is occupied and added to by each succeeding generation.

Some of our traditions are designed to ensure our survival, but more of them are engineered to socialise us into communities, turning the guttural wails of an infant into the attuned etiquette of an adult. Etiquette in its broadest sense is concerned with the common courtesies of social discourse which our parents inculcate in us from a very young age.

Predominantly, etiquette is about accommodation and compromise with those around us. It is a tacit language which makes our lives and the lives of our fellow citizens as pleasant as possible in the routine of our regular social intercourse. The commonality of etiquette also indicates that tradition is a shared civic enterprise which fortifies the bonds of a community.

Yet, beyond trivial traditions which regulate the routine of a community, there are deeper traditions which *define what we are*. The philosopher Sir Roger Scruton makes the important point that 'we may not be consciously aware of these traditions, but they determine our primary responses, what we do and how we do it, when reacting to others around us.'[136]

Our most deeply held values are usually hidden from view in our everyday lives, but they occasionally surface, like giants from the deep, to express themselves in traditions of social ritual. We might think of marriage, funerary rites, graduation ceremonies, Remembrance Sunday, military commissioning parades, the opening of parliament or the coronation of a monarch. Such traditions are formalised expressions of acts which are significant in the life of a community. As such, they are usually endowed with a solemnity that is appropriate for the occasion and serve to encapsulate core social values, inviting those present to partake in the explicit reaffirmation of those things which undergird our shared lives.

As Scruton points out, ritual tells you that 'what you are doing is not done only by you, [but] that your choice must be sanctified by the community.'[137] In such moments we encounter the intersection between the mundane and the sacred. The functionalist explanations of ritual offered by anthropologists are useful in helping us to dissect such occasions, but we need not be constrained by the secularist assumptions they often presuppose. For those who are religious, such rituals offer moments in which the life of the community touches the divine, revitalising their shared life as they encounter the transcendent within their own cultural context. The feeling that we are encountering something that transcends time links us with our ancestors, reaffirming the enduring nature of our fundamental beliefs and realigning our moral bearings; all of this serves to bring that which is beyond our own direct experience into *our* history. As Burke wrote, 'each contract of each particular state is but a clause in the great primaeval contract of eternal society, linking the lower with the higher nature, connecting the visible and invisible world.'

Tradition as something given

Twentieth century phenomenologists, such as Edmund Husserl and Martin Heidegger reflected on the remarkable fact that each one of us has been flung into *being* inside a universe that existed before our eyes ever opened for the first time. It is a fact that perhaps we do not spend much time reflecting on, but we enter the great narrative of existence after many volumes have already been written. We enter into a world which is given to us in an existential sense but, as humans, we also enter into a world that is gifted to us in an intellectual sense, through the great heritage of thought and experience that our species has cultivated.

In Thomas Hardy's *Jude the Obscure,* the main character, Jude, stands at a crossroads in Christminster (Hardy's cipher for Oxford) and reflects on all the events that have transpired at the very spot on which he stands. Jude had:

> fallen into thought on what struggling people like himself had stood at that Crossway, whom nobody ever thought of now… At fourways men had stood and talked of Napoleon, the loss of America, the execution of King Charles, the burning of the Martyrs, the Crusades, the Norman Conquest, possibly of the arrival of Caesar. Here the two sexes had met for loving, hating, coupling, parting, had waited, had suffered for each other.[138]

Many of us will, like Jude, have stood at an old monument and been struck by all the human experience that has taken place there and marvelled at how it might have shaped the world we now live in. Such reflections should lead to the humbling realisation that the social structures and technological achievements that sustain us are an invaluable heritage gifted to us.

Understanding that as individuals we are not the authors of our own success, but the recipients of the bounty won by past generations is at the heart of conservatism. Among all creatures on earth, we are the great inheritors.

Our intellect as *homo sapiens* has allowed us to store vast amounts of information and pass this from one generation to the next. If our shared knowledge was lost between generations then we might be thrown back into the half light of the pre-literate Palaeolithic age. This realisation ought to induce humility in us and a deep attentiveness to the past. In a rapidly changing world, full of remarkable new technologies, there is a temptation to believe that we owe nothing to former generations. In reality we too stand on the shoulders of giants. As the famous composer Gustav Mahler argued, 'Tradition is not the worship of ashes, but the preservation of fire.'

Traditions therefore are not just intellectual truths that are given to us, but they are the social patterns which, whether we know it or not, tacitly transform us into individuals who are fitted for participation in a complex world. They teach us 'not only about who we [are], but also about who we [can] become'.[139] This process synchronises each generation with the story of their community and poises them to make their own contribution to the evolving social body.

Tradition and politics

Political authority in Britain rests on the marriage of tradition and democratically mandated power. Tradition does not make political authority irrational, but rather it gives a historical weight to our political forms, which is tethered to the story of our community. Tradition and power are wedded, because in order for a people to corporately mandate power to their government, they must have a shared history. They may disagree on the details of the next leg of the journey, but they are more likely to disagree amicably if they have walked the last legs together. Moreover, they ought to feel that they are penning the next chapter of a national story, which extends back into the immemorial past. Burke made this point when he wrote 'people will not look forward to posterity who never look backward to their ancestors'.[140]

This national journey of shared conversations, internal wrestling and corporate acts of election, makes the difference between *a* government and *my* government. In a democracy that relies on participation, this is an important distinction. As we have seen, traditions offer a recurrent snapshot of this shared narrative, through symbolism and social syntax.

The corporate story which is conveyed through traditions requires a stage, a locality, in which it is played out. It is possible that a people may be divorced from a geographical locality for a time but, as the story of the Jews has illustrated for four thousand years, the identity of a people is almost always envisaged in relation to a homeland. Even if a community is driven from its locality, its traditions often remain bound up with the memory of that locality; the Jewish Diaspora and the Islamic Ummah both offer a good case in point. We have seen the importance of a nation state in a previous chapter, but we should note the way in which tradition plays a crucial role in sustaining the nexus of behaviours, habits, language and ideas which constitute a nation's culture. By sustaining the idea of the nation, tradition plays an important role in invigorating democracy and maintaining stability.

Not only is our political freedom enhanced by tradition but our personal freedom (which includes our self realisation in a community) relies upon the existence of traditions. Oliver O'Donovan notes:

> For Greeks to be free implies not merely that they can live in Greece and communicate with other people there; but that they can receive from previous generations of Greeks accumulated stores of experience and practice related to the place, and can contribute constructively to younger Greeks… as we discover the extent of what we have received, we recognise the significance of our social identity.[141]

We have seen how law is a necessary condition for freedom, because it allows us to live an ordered life within community. But equally important is the identity that a particular community impresses upon us. We are all shaped by the culture that we grow up in. A healthy culture gifts us with the treasures that have accumulated in that society, which will include everything from playwrights and philosophers to less tangible goods, such as a particular brand of humour.[142] All of these things are stepping stones in our journey to becoming a self reflective and healthily functioning human being.

If we are to resist a government exercising a totalitarian claim upon its citizens, it is important to recognise that we are not identical to our culture. In other words, we must preserve space for individuals to discover their own vocation. It is the role of society to edify us, raise us and enlarge us until we can think for ourselves and realise our own ambitions and potential. It is at this point that philosophical and spiritual perspectives allow us to critically reflect upon and reform the society which we came from.[143]

The heterogeneity of the world means that the process of individual formation and social reformation can be enacted in a wide variety of different contexts. The experience of a Spaniard will not be that of a Scandinavian. Such heterogeneity is welcomed by conservatives. Yet, some societies are clearly more successful at equipping their citizens with the tools they need to be fulfilled human beings than others.[144] The extent to which a society is equipped for this task will depend upon the extent to which a society offers an authentic vision of reality. It is only through an accurate perception of the world that a citizen is able to critically reflect upon the society they have come from. The most extreme failure of this process occurs under the rule of totalitarian states, such as North Korea, where the individual can never be conceived of as separate from the state. Under such circumstances, not only does the individual never develop, but the state ossifies with little means of evolution other than by mandate from the top.

Tradition and Place

The fact that traditions are a product of place is an affront to the liberal idea that fundamentally we are all cosmopolitan citizens of the world. The power of tradition upon our personal formation is a reminder that we are not *just* humans with rights, but we are shaped by our localities in ways that are both psychologically and ethically significant.

As much as liberal political theory has a penchant for speaking of humans abstractly, as bearers of natural rights, these are a mirage without a political territory in which to delineate, assert and defend these rights.

In 1215, central principles of English law were enacted in a charter which influences our nation and other English speaking countries to this day. King John of England arrived at the small village of Runnymede to parley with his insurrectionary barons. Yet the document he signed has almost nothing in it which we find in the great documents of liberty, revered by liberals. Unlike the French revolutionaries' *Declaration on the Rights of Man*, the Great Charter of 1215 has no sweeping pronouncement concerning the manifest rights which every human possesses. In fact, it is much more modest. But in its modesty lies its beauty, because it is a document authored by a people who treasured their customary rights and who knew the character of their nation. Demanding a general right to liberty is so vague as to mean almost nothing, but demanding that the king refrain from arbitrary detention without trial, limit taxation and honour the customary rights of towns represents a statement of the very specific liberties which meant freedom to a medieval Englishman. Magna Carta was asking that 'men of our kingdom' should have their 'liberties and free customs' given to them as they were due 'according to the ancient and rightful customs'.

The customary rights of Englishmen, claimed in the Magna Carta, were not the modern innovation of universal and subjectively held natural rights proposed by Rousseau, Diderot and Voltaire; they were contextual, sensitive to circumstance and rooted in tradition. They were rights that emerged from a place.

This precise point was made by Edmund Burke when radical English liberals sought to undermine the constitution on the basis of universal rights:

> You will observe, that from Magna Carta to the Declaration of Right, it has been the uniform policy of our constitution to claim and assert our liberties, *as an entailed inheritance* derived to us from our forefathers, and to be transmitted to our posterity; as an estate especially belonging to the people of this kingdom without any reference whatever to any other more general or prior right.[145]

The same point was recognised by Benjamin Disraeli as he saw Europe wracked by the turbulence born of abstract philosophical rights which sought to dissolve ancient order and inherited tradition. He wrote: 'To the liberalism they profess, I prefer the liberty we enjoy; to the Rights of Man, the rights of Englishmen'.

Common law rights are not the inalienable rights proposed by modern liberals, such as the ostensible human right to family life. To think of us simply as bearers of rights, outside of community and outside of legal structures is a category error, since it applies a legal lexicon (that is contingent upon legal structures) to a theological truth: that we are created with an inherent value and dignity. Further, the idea of natural rights is particularly incoherent outside of a broader theological context, specifically the idea of a creator and a natural order.

Politically, the danger of this philosophical confusion is that it risks undermining the very real necessity for the communities, laws and traditions which secure a tangible recognition of our dignity. The mistake of 17th century liberal theorists such as John Locke and his epigones was to suppose that humans in a state of nature should be conceived of as antecedent to communities and laws; an idea which led to revolutionaries being swept away by the power of their own revolutions. Rather than try to reform existing constitutions and legal systems, the revolutionaries of eighteenth and nineteenth century Europe often tore down the bulwarks of the actual legal rights they possessed. The result in the French revolution was tyranny and chaos. Tradition gives our rights a deep historical grounding which helps to secure them by rooting them in our national story.

Tradition and the modern world

In a world of iPhones and air travel, it is easy to believe that local and even national traditions might dissipate with the frenetic pace and connectivity of the modern world. Yet, such trends are not as easy to predict as we might assume. As we have seen, traditions are more than just beliefs or propositions, they are also modes of being and acting which are woven into the fabric of our communities in subtle ways that we may not even be aware of.

Friedrich Hayek argued that traditions will survive because of their utility. Using a Darwinist vocabulary, Hayek made the point that traditions which did not serve a purpose or express some truth which played a role in the life of the community were discarded for precisely that reason. Mutations which prove successful in a new environment will inevitably prosper. Tradition has always been the meeting of history and imagination: social truths encapsulated in ritual.

The inherent human craving for narrative continuity and a connection with the past will very likely continue to assert itself, though this may happen in unexpected and unpredictable ways. Doubtless, some of these ways will use modern innovations. The conversation between the customary and the contemporary is a dialectic which drives change.

Perhaps unexpectedly, there has been a revival of historical traditions in Britain over the last fifteen years. In the same way that the nation state has reasserted itself, against all expectations, traditional identities have also emerged with a new vigour, old but *avant-garde*. One example of this is found in traditional folk music. Bands such as *Mumford and Sons, Johnny Flynn* and *Noah and the Whale* have used modern mediums to produce a variation on a traditional style. Some traditional activities have subsided as they have diminished in relevance, such as burning a Guy on Guy Fawkes Night, but other traditions have grown exponentially (often abetted by marketing and overseas influences), such as the celebration of Halloween.

A number of organisations which promote national traditions are also flourishing. Amongst young people, the popularity of The Scouts is at an all time high in Britain with over half a million members. It is an organisation replete with tradition, yet it has repeatedly reinvented itself for a new generation, offering engaging activities, opening up membership to girls and dispensing of those elements of the uniform which were seen as outdated. Television programmes such as *The Great British Bake Off* have given traditional hobbies a new lease of life and captivated a new generation.

Even more notable, has been the success of period dramas such as *Downton Abbey* in which people are offered an insight into, even a connection with, the traditions of the past. It is not a coincidence that such interest in period dramas has coincided with membership of the National Trust reaching an all time high, with over 4.5 million members visiting heritage properties.

In terms of the symbolic significance of our national traditions, international support for the British monarchy has never been higher, with over two billion people watching the Royal Wedding of William and Kate in 2011. The monarchy is paradigmatic of an institution which carries all the symbolic gravity of the past and yet is willing to shed some outmoded customs in order to remain relevant.

Our personal sense of heritage has also peaked. Concurrent with the rise of technology over the last two decades, there has been an enormous rise in interest in family genealogies. The website Ancestry.com was launched in 1996; since that time the brand has achieved enormous success, attracting millions of customers worldwide. In 2012, they expanded to genome testing, in order to help customers discover their ethnic origins. The interest in ancestors has been publicised in television programmes such as *Who Do You Think You Are?* in which individuals discover the story of their ancestors with the help of history experts. Such a fascination with ancestry has transformed our understanding of ourselves and is likely to perpetuate traditions which we feel link us with our ancestors. Importantly, it shows that the impulse to know *who* we are and where we are from is as strong as ever.

Culture

Culture is a term that has eluded a satisfactory definition; like many concepts, it is easily recognised in particular instances, but hard to identify in its essence. Rather than discussing abstractions, it may be helpful to explore the history of the term.

The etymology of the word is classical in its origins. It arrived in the English language from the Medieval Latin word *Culturare*, which derived from the Latin *Colere* meaning to cultivate. The connection with our modern usage arises from a metaphor developed in the sixteenth century, in which it was humans rather than agriculture who were cultivated. The idea of humans being grown from their native soil remains a useful analogy for our understanding of culture.

The term only took on its modern meaning, as a noun, during the nineteenth century in the work of the German Romantics. In 1772 Johann Gottfried Herder sought to offer an account of the origins of language and culture.[146] Herder, for the first time, made the case that language shapes our social structures and even moulds the way we think. Language is therefore responsible for producing distinct human cultures.

Wilhelm von Humboldt developed the work of Herder, developing linguistics in a more scientific fashion. He believed that the 'inner life' of a community was embodied in its language. For both of these men, culture was a social act in which an individual thinks and behaves in a manner characteristic of the group to which they belong. In this view we can easily detect resonances of the patriotic conception of the German *Volk*.

This account of culture was picked up on by the anthropologists and sociologists of the late nineteenth and early twentieth centuries. Georg Simmel drew attention to culture as the shared aspects of our social existence, which forms us as individuals, while Durkheim drew attention to the fact that culture has an intellectual component as well as a functional component, which shapes our view of the world. In particular he explored the social rites of our societies. Perhaps the most influential definition of culture was offered by Clifford Geertz in the 1970s. He spoke of culture as a 'system of inherited conceptions expressed in symbolic forms by means of which men communicate, perpetuate, and develop their knowledge about and attitudes towards life'.[147]

Quite separately, there was an account of culture being developed in the English speaking world, which emphasised the cream of a nation's attainments: what we might today call 'high culture'. Matthew Arnold was the chief advocate of this interpretation of culture. In it, he was followed by notable conservatives such as T. S. Eliot. Both accounts of culture are helpful as we explore its role in our society. To break this broad topic down we will split it into two categories: popular culture and high culture.

Popular Culture

Conservatives believe that culture is at least as important as the politics of a nation, because in large part it determines a nation's politics. Yet, in spite of its importance, it receives little academic attention, in comparison with either politics or economics. As one commentator notes, 'culture is difficult to quantify, and operates in a highly complex context with psychological, institutional, political, geographic, and other factors'.[148]

In his *Reflections on the Revolution in France* Edmund Burke spoke of the 'manners' of a nation, which he claimed 'engages the mind in a steady course of wisdom and virtue'. Customs, then, are standards of behaviour which embody the wisdom of previous generations. Why do we value politeness? Why do we respect our elders? We are taught these habits of custom, because they are founded on the good sense of experience. While custom offers us unspoken modes of acceptable conduct, it is also contextual, conforming to the temperament of a people. For example, the British habit of queuing in silence for service may not appeal to people of a more extroverted culture, who might behave differently.

Like Herder, many conservatives believe that the way in which groups behave is inextricably linked with the implicit values and aspirations of that group. The temper of a nation is directly related to the smaller units of family and tribe. For instance, in the 1970s Japan created an extensive system of welfare which produced impressive results despite a significantly lower level of expenditure than Western nations. This was achieved because the Japanese people had a strong sense of familial duty and community. Companies and communities continued to care for the elderly and provide workplace pensions long after the state offered to fund these services. In Britain and America, the welfare state ballooned over the same period of time, in large part because the West's ethos of individualism meant that people did not have the same networks of familial support, or the same reservations about accepting free provision from the state.[149] This is illustrated by the stark contrast in the numbers that utilised the offer of state welfare. By 1996 only 0.7 per cent of Japanese citizens received benefits, compared with 9.7 per cent of Americans who were on food stamps, not to mention other forms of welfare.[150]

Beyond the immediate customs and rules of conduct in a society, culture also entails ethical and religious attitudes. How do we as a nation reason ethically? In what story is our self-understanding situated? Narrative plays a crucial role in the process of self-understanding and ascertaining values. For example, Native American Cherokee tribesmen in the nineteenth century would have known the narrative of Unetlanvhi as a great creator, or the Thunders who supposedly brought rain and lightning to the land, because these concepts furnished a basis for their self understanding and their conception of the natural world. Such stories profoundly shape the values and beliefs that a people hold about themselves.

Herder presents us with one more important idea. The acceptance of a common political power must be based on a common culture. This idea accords with a number of political thinkers, as diverse as Aristotle, Cicero, John of Salisbury and John Fortescue, all of who use the metaphor of the head being a natural extension of the body. The political is an extension of the social; where culture is discordant, politics will amplify these tensions.

High Culture

Roger Scruton writes 'A high culture is the self-consciousness of a society. It contains the works of art, literature, scholarship and philosophy that establish a shared frame of reference among educated people.'[151] High culture can be seen as the essence of a society, a distillation of its core values and talents. As such, it is developed over the course of generations, as a gradual and organic extension of the social order on which it rests. Like Isaac Newton, who famously said that he stood on the shoulders of giants, so high culture is developed over centuries and crowns the cultural achievements of a civilisation. For instance, the sophists of Athenian antiquity may never have achieved their high philosophy outside of the democratic structures of Athenian society, just as the architects of Rome emerged from a society of order, grandiosity and education.

While high culture is a reflection of society, it also has the power to influence, innovate and alter the form of our current culture. High culture may be a possession of a relatively small proportion of the population, just as the highest echelons of any academic study are, but at its best it has the ability to enrich popular culture and infiltrate into society in myriad ways; so we find shades of Hamlet in The Lion King and Beethoven in The Beatles. In other words, there is a reciprocity between high culture and popular culture.

Matthew Arnold wrote that culture was the 'great help out of our present difficulties'. Just as scientists at the very top of their field occasionally have great creative leaps forward, so Arnold believed that through a knowledge of 'the best that has been thought and said in the world', we might generate a 'stream of fresh and free thought upon our stock notions and habits'.[152] For Arnold, high culture was a study of perfection and its end result was an alteration in the human mind and spirit, which moved people to 'leave the world better and happier than we found it'. In his mind, the pursuit of perfection militates against the selfish individualism within humanity and points us towards reason. In this sense there is a visionary element to high culture which, at times, critiques and chastises the society from which it has emerged. This prophetic capacity of culture is the reason that some of the provocative art, literature and music of today could come to be the high culture of tomorrow; so it was with John Bunyan, William Blake and Søren Kierkegaard.

T. S. Eliot and Christian culture

Perhaps the most important conservative account of culture was offered by T. S. Eliot. Eliot saw liberalism as the great enemy of culture in Britain. He argued that it was corrosive of social traditions and cultural cohesion. In his view, it told citizens that they were individuals and sought to dissolve their sense of collective identity. He warned that societies which lose their moral cohesion eventually dissolve into anarchy. This anarchy produces a reaction of totalitarianism.

For Eliot the dominant culture that holds British society together is Christianity. In *The Idea of A Christian Society* he writes:

> The Liberal notion that religion was a matter of private belief and of conduct in private life, and that there is no reason why Christians should not be able to accommodate themselves to any world which treats them good-naturedly, is becoming less and less tenable.

Eliot was prescient in seeing that the seemingly virtuous push for toleration in liberalism has the capacity to create a nihilistic culture of its own, focused on absolute licence; before long, people would be subject to this culture, whether they liked it or not. The implicit presumptions of society would all militate against faith.

T. S. Eliot saw the beginning of the decline of Christianity in Britain. It troubled him greatly as he observed that the British people still lived with the vestiges of a Christian culture in the symbols they used to make sense of the world, in their ethical norms and in the cultural fabric of Britain itself. Eliot is one among many who have argued that religion brings to culture a public morality which is essential to the preservation of liberty. In fact, before the twentieth century any other presumption can hardly be found in Anglophone political thought. It is a theme that is consistently reiterated by the United States founding fathers. Samuel Adams wrote:

> A general dissolution of principles and manners will more surely overthrow the liberties of America than the whole force of the common enemy. While the people are virtuous they cannot be subdued; but when once they lose their virtue then will be ready to surrender their liberties to the first external or internal invader.

We should however be wary, as Eliot was, of making religion synonymous with culture, as an absolute elision can damage both enterprises. Where this occurs, culture can find itself overly moralistic, sanctified and immune from critique, while religion can find itself endowing a national enterprise with legitimacy.[153] Alive to this danger, Eliot pointed out that 'elements of local culture – even of local barbarism – may become invested with the sanctity of religious observances'. For Eliot, religion had the dual role of informing but also of critiquing culture 'in and out of season'; if it does not do so, 'the world will constantly confuse the right with the expedient'.[154]

Culture Wars

In 1991, James Davison Hunter published *Culture Wars: The Struggle to Define America*. He identified that there was increasingly a contest for cultural influence between two groups with widely different approaches to a number of contemporary issues. He characterised the dichotomy as one between 'orthodoxy' and 'progressivism'.[155] Today we can see the hallmarks of this culture war, which is often played out in the media or the arts.

One problem with such a battle is that it ends up polarising debate as each side vies for the dominance of their worldview. The BBC news, for instance, is replete with daily editorials on issues of gender identity and sexuality. The concentration on these issues is out of all proportion to the number of people promoting them and in no way reflects the broad interests of the nation. It is hard to draw any other conclusion than that they are designed to serve a didactic ethical function, telling the people of the nation what they ought to believe.

We have already touched upon the fact that there is a general fear pervading the populace when it comes to challenging the claims of militant liberals. There is a very real prospect of losing one's job, or even being reported to the police for professing what, until recently, would be considered reasonable views. A statistically small, yet vocal and powerful minority has successfully wielded culture as a weapon. Instead of culture reflecting a people's character it is increasingly becoming a tool of social control. This is an ever increasing danger in a digitalised, consumer society in which trending opinions are marketable. An emerging opinion can take hold extremely quickly, sometimes before a proper public debate has ever taken place.

When subjective feelings are allowed to trump empirical realities, then there are no longer any objectively discernible norms by which a society can be run. This is a phenomenon increasingly prevalent in the law. Causing offence can now be regarded as an assault. In other words, a crime is not just concerned with what has actually been said or done; it is contingent on how it has been received.[156]

The best option available to conservatives is to publicly counter liberalism with reasonable argument and empirical evidence, thereby exposing those areas where liberal dogma is vacuous. In the long run this will dislodge its pretence of reasonableness and show it for what it is. If conservatives allow themselves to be cowed by the pitch of hysteria with which criticism of liberalism is often met, then deference to the shrillest voice will continue.

Perhaps the best hope for our culture is the common sense of ordinary people taking a stand against ideologically driven oppression. In response to the revolutionary liberals in nineteenth century Britain, Edmund Burke wrote:

Because half a dozen grasshoppers under a fern make the field ring with their importunate chink, whilst thousands of great cattle, reposed beneath the shadow of the British oak, chew the cud and are silent, pray do not imagine that those who make the noise are the only inhabitants of the field.

His words would be well heeded today.

Chapter Seven

RELIGION

The real crisis we face today is a spiritual one; at root, it is a test of moral will and faith – Ronald Reagan

Aristotle rightly assumed politics to be a branch of ethics. Politics is by its very nature a facet of our ethical life as it is concerned with the pursuit of a perceived set of normative social goods. Even if all of the decisions made in everyday governance are not strictly ethical, the thrust of their intent ought to aim for ethical ends.

It is for this reason that religion is both the start and the end of political theory. Its narratives shape our most foundational beliefs about the world, from which we extrapolate ethical and political principles. As a result its gravity has a firm hold upon each of the other topics that we have looked at.

For many, there will be unease about the fraternisation of religion and politics. There is a legitimate anxiety that we should hold about the functional links between religious and secular institutions. As Burke once wrote 'politics and the pulpit are terms that have little agreement'. Historically, when religious authorities have assumed political rule, it has often led to religious oppression. But this is very different from the legitimate commerce that exists between religious belief and political judgements.[157] In other words, there is no reason that an electorate, or a political leader, should attempt to divorce their political reason from the substantive claims of their religion. As Reagan put it:

When our Founding Fathers passed the First Amendment, they sought to protect churches from government interference. They never meant to construct a wall of hostility between government and the concept of religious belief itself.[158]

127

Such an intellectual partition was the project pioneered by the French *philosophes*, with their advocacy of a politics governed by pure reason. This foundationalist epistemology was discredited in political theory by Burke, shortly before it was discredited in practice by the collapse of social order in France. If our religious beliefs illuminate our most profoundly held convictions, such as the sanctity of human life and the existence of a moral law, then it would be illogical not to see them as the conceptual framework for our politics.

Both liberalism and socialism have sought to exorcise religious belief from politics in their own way. This was an idea famously expressed by Tony Blair's spin doctor, Alistair Campbell, who said 'we don't do God'. By contrast, Johnson, Disraeli, Salisbury and other leading figures of the conservative tradition have followed Burke in arguing that the functional separation of institutions does not preclude religion occupying a central role in our civil and political life.[159]

Indeed, it was these deep religious convictions that motivated William Wilberforce to end the slave trade and Salisbury to alleviate the plight of the poor. Wilberforce claimed that 'the suppression of the slave trade' was one of the 'great objects' that 'God Almighty has set before [him]', and he consistently made the case for abolition on biblical grounds. Similarly, Salisbury defended his Housing of the Working Class Bill, by arguing that it was 'derived from the noblest principles of philanthropy and religion'.[160]

Christianity and Conservatism

No party has a monopoly on religious truth, but some political theories are logically derived from, and consistent with, religious beliefs. Conservatism is a body of political conclusions that has been constructed within the scaffolding of the Christian tradition. Christianity does not give us a political model, but it does offer an account of the nature of the universe we live in. From the Christian doctrine of original sin comes the conservative scepticism of utopian ideologies; from the Christian belief in human finitude comes the conservative belief in conservation; from the Christian commendation of justice comes the conservative care for the poor; and from the Christian belief in a divinely ordered universe comes the conservative belief in the rule of law.

A full exposition of the theological foundations of conservatism has been done in depth elsewhere.[161] But the seminal text of conservatism, Edmund Burke's *Reflections on the Revolution in France*, is a political tract inseparable from its religious vision. In Burke's eyes it was not just the law of man, but the law of God that the revolutionaries were violating. If *Reflections* is concerned with a contract between the living, the dead and future generations, it is equally concerned with the contract between Heaven and Earth.

Yet, while conservatism does emerge from a religious logic, it has embraced individuals from all faiths and none. One does not need to be a Christian to be a conservative. But because conservatism's political prescriptions bear fidelity to reality, its fruits commend themselves on their own merits irrespective of whether an individual accepts the religious roots which formed them.

Christianity and British Society

For over a millennium Christianity has been the dominant ethical force in both European and Anglo-Saxon civilisations. Christianity first arrived on the shores of Great Britain in the Roman period. The gospel was likely transmitted to the extremities of Great Britain through the great vascular network of the Roman Empire, surviving in some areas following the departure of the Romans. During the Saxon period, the Gregorian mission to Britain made a significant impact upon the nation, converting much of southern Britain and establishing bishoprics and an ecclesial hierarchy in the country. In the ninth century, Alfred the Great, King of Wessex, made it is his life mission to convert the nation of England to Christianity. By the time of his great grandson Edgar's coronation in the city of Bath (973 AD), England was a Christian country, with a network of monasteries propagating Christian teaching.

Since that time, the Christian faith has defined many of our basic ethical ideas about the world: the pre-eminence of grace, sanctification and redemption, the belief that all humans have intrinsic worth, the concept of monogamous marital commitment and, perhaps most fundamentally, the idea that rulers are accountable before the law, as it is not created by them, but by God. While it is true that some of these beliefs have arisen in other cultures, they are by no means universal.

The intellectual transition from Christianity to secular liberalism is a longer and more complex story, but it is a story worth recounting in brief. In the seventeenth century the veracity of religious belief was publicly questioned for the first time in Christian Europe. The Dutch Jew Spinoza asked whether God's moral law was not in fact constraining humanity, rather than liberating it. In England, Thomas Hobbes, who earned the sobriquet 'the monster of Malmesbury' due to his suspected atheism, was penning his *Leviathan*, which seemed to portray humans as animals, with little hint of the divine signature. In the eighteenth century, Immanuel Kant attempted to place religious morality on the footing of rationalism, but arguably only succeeded in thinning religious truths into rational dictums, which were repudiated by subsequent thinkers.

By the nineteenth century the philosophical atheism of Nietzsche boldly declared that God was dead, though Nietzsche did not necessarily welcome this grand realisation, perturbed at the idea it would untether society from all its moral anchors: 'are we not straying as through an infinite nothing?'.[162] In 1867 Matthew Arnold wrote his poem *Dover Beach,* in which he captured the intellectual *zeitgeist*. He speaks of the 'melancholy, long withdrawing roar' of the 'sea of faith' which was once 'at the full', but has now receded to expose the 'naked shingles of the world'. The profound anxieties, which still existed in Enlightenment thinkers, as to where human morality would come from, were for many satisfied by the hedonic calculus of Jeremy Bentham's utilitarianism, later refined by John Stuart Mill. The created order of divinely ordained ends had evaporated, leaving only pleasure and pain as the sole arbiter of the good.

This line of moral thought would resurface in Britain in the 1960s. Twentieth century emotivists such as A. J. Ayer and C. L. Stevenson argued that moral language represents simply expressions of approval or disapproval, as opposed to meaningful propositions. Similarly, the logical positivists based in Berlin and Vienna held that the only meaningful propositions were those which were empirically verifiable or analytically self-evident, thus relegating all metaphysics, aesthetics and ethics to meaninglessness. The transition from the belief in an objective moral order to ethical subjectivity and moral relativism was complete.

The twentieth century also saw the culmination of the intellectual drift towards atheism. The existentialism of Jean-Paul Sartre picked up on Nietzsche's conclusions. He saw humans as beings thrown into a godless universe, 'condemned to be free'. For the first time the onus was thrown onto humanity to forge meaning in a meaningless world.

The concurrent and seemingly inexorable rise of science served to harry religion from much of its traditional territory. The rise of Darwinian evolutionary theory in the biological sciences ousted God as the only explanation for the complexity of biological beings and simultaneously displaced humans from their exalted status in the hierarchy of creation. No longer could Christian apologists such as William Paisley use the intricacy of biological life to assert intelligent design. The rise of Freudian psychology argued that the human proclivity towards belief in God was based upon the infantile desire for a paternal figure. While such religion had a role to play in primitive societies, it had been rendered nugatory in an age of reason. Concurrently, the early anthropologists such as Bronislaw Malinowski and Émile Durkheim were explaining the role of religion in terms of social cohesion, reducing it to a purely functionalist explanation for the coherence of primitive societies. Of all the sciences it was perhaps only physics, in its astonishing leaps forward during the twentieth century, which served to deepen rather than dissipate the mysteries of the universe in the popular imagination.

In the political realm, Lockean liberalism, which had never successfully usurped Britain's constitutional Christianity, reasserted itself in the 1948 Universal Declaration of Human Rights, masterminded by Franklin D. Roosevelt. In 1998 the UK passed the Human Rights Act which incorporated the European Convention on Human Rights (1953) into UK law. Since this time, the Human Rights Act has given a new account of the human person to the citizens of the UK, helping to reshape the moral landscape of the nation around a secular code of rights. This was a subtle yet important contrast to the rights enshrined in the common law and a culture in which duty, rather than rights, was paramount.

Beyond the intellectual and political background that we have looked at, there are a number of deep social currents which led to this shift. The sociological explanations for the transition to a more secularised and liberal public discourse have focused on the proliferation of different religions,[163] the rise of technology and mass media, the consumerism that accompanies an advanced capitalist economy,[164] and the conscious advancement of a secular liberal discourse by Western intellectuals.[165]

From that brief romp through the highlands of modern history, we might be deceived into believing that Britain has been an irreligious place for quite some time. In reality, until the relatively recent past (around the late 1960s) Britain had high levels of religiosity and the cultural discourse of the nation was dominated by the Christian religion. Our language, our names, our buildings, our parliament, our law and our ideas were all deeply impressed with the hallmarks of the Christian faith; moral debate was publicly conducted in relation to Christian moral principles and the Church played a leading role in the social and political life of the nation.

The problem

In modern Britain a number of prominent religious voices now feel that faith is increasingly marginalised in the public square. Secular liberalism now dominates our society. The result has been a number of flashpoint issues which have caused significant tensions with religious communities.

To take one issue, the Catholic Church, in common with other Christians, teaches that human life is endowed with a special sanctity and it starts at conception. As a result, many Christians are horrified by the abortion clinics which together terminate hundreds of thousands of pregnancies a year. For some Christians this is morally indistinguishable from genocide of the innocent. Yet, for most secular liberals, the maximisation of a woman's autonomy is the salient matter in question.

In October 2009, in Spain, over a million people marched through the streets of Madrid to oppose the proposed liberalisation of Spanish abortion laws, in a demonstration that was backed by prominent bishops and politicians. Similarly, every year on the 22nd January there is a mass march through Washington D. C. in order to lament the anniversary of the Supreme Court Judgement (Roe vs Wade) that first legalised abortion.

Such questions are not empirical issues that can be resolved by recourse to science or abstract logic alone, rather they are issues which, in large part, depend on the way that we see the world and the narratives we believe. If, in the modern world, legislative programmes are increasingly disparate, or there seems to be an increasing inability to find any point of connection between different political positions, it seems that this is symptomatic of a more tectonic shift, as the fundamental truths we believe in are ever more divergent.

Where liberalism began in the seventeenth century as a Christian plea for toleration, it soon metamorphosed into a creed of its own. In our culture today there are a number of senior religious figures who fear this creed is at risk of marginalising the horizon of religious conscience which exists beyond secular reason.[166] Rather than protecting those of religious faith by asserting a robust case for freedom of religious conscience, secular liberalism is increasingly a prescriptive system of belief in itself.

Modern secular liberalism has a very definite set of philosophical assumptions which have worked their way into everything from the BBC News to school and university curriculums. It posits a society of individuals who are defined by their lack of conformity; in other words, they are radically free to be whatever or whoever they want to be. Liberal secularism tells us we have absolute choice over our identity; it scorns traditional institutions and is often supercilious towards religious claims; and its fundamental belief is that humans are solitary rights bearers, not morally ordered beings with a higher purpose.

The question for many religious citizens has been whether liberalism's belief in humans as autonomous bearers of rights is not just another faith tradition in the competing market of faiths? Why should this tradition receive a public privilege, when its founding myth seems to bear very little relation to any historical fact?

Even non-religious individuals are questioning the dubious story that liberalism tells. Yuval Noah Harari correctly perceived that the myth of rational and free agency pedalled by liberalism is, in the end, historically, biologically and psychologically false: 'the free individual is just a fictional tale'. Harari informs his readers that 'we will probably require a brand-new package of religious beliefs and political institutions'.[167] He is correct that it is hard to claim liberalism's ideas are 'reasonable' outside of any convincing narrative. Even beyond the doubtful historicity of liberalism's claims, philosophers such as Ludwig Wittgenstein perceived long ago that moral reasonability is contingent upon the prior commitments of a community and cannot simply be arrived at by reason detached from tradition.

The hope that a secular creed such as liberalism can impartially defend religious belief more effectively than an established religion may prove naïve. History would suggest that any secular ideology which occupies the heart of our social existence will end up transforming itself into an object of veneration. Burke observed that man is 'by his constitution a religious animal'; similarly Disraeli wrote that 'the most powerful principle which governs man is the religious principle'. Fascists worshipped the nation state, just as communists worshipped the party. It is telling that, in instigating the Bolshevik Revolution, Lenin urged his followers to revolution, calling it a 'holy war'. Similarly, the French revolutionaries ended up making a cult of reason, seeking to purge any religion that conflicted with their liberalism. G.K. Chesterton observed that when men cease to believe in God, they don't believe in nothing, they believe in anything. We should be vigilant to ensure that liberalism does not once again become an oppressive faith.

A shared moral vision

The British people seem to have decided that their moral reason has outgrown what liberals regard as the infantility of religion. Christianity is dying in Britain, not with a bang but with a whimper. Britain is already a *de facto* secular nation, in terms of formal religious affiliation. According to a 2017 NatCen social attitudes survey in 2017, 53% of British adults described themselves as having no religious affiliation.[165] If Britain continues on its current trajectory, Christianity will be entirely extinct in Britain by 2067.[169] If this trend persists, Britain will discover the fruits of this change for good or ill.

If it is true that, in order to thrive, a society needs a set of basic unifying assumptions, it should be a cause of concern that we are losing the moral canopy of ideas and symbols which historically united our nation. The social psychologist Jonathan Haidt has pointed out the importance of morality in binding groups together.[170] At the most basic level the shared life of a community presupposes a shared set of assumptions; a shared moral vision. I use the term moral vision, because morality must consist in more than a code. It must emerge from the narrative and self-understanding of a people. People adhere to moral norms, not because they have been dictated to them, but because adherence to them is central to their identity as a people.

An example of this is found in the most ancient and enduring human community on earth, the Jewish people. The Shema is a passage in Hebrew Scripture, in which God addresses the Jewish people and gives them a series of commandments as a preface to their moral law.

This moral law is not given abstractly, but rather their moral identity is connected to their narrative identity. The people are commanded to Love the LORD their God with all their heart and with all their soul and with all their strength. They are told to make the commandments a part of their everyday lives, they are to impress them on their children, talk about them when they sit at home and when they walk along the road, when they lie down and when they get up. They are reminded of all that God has given to them: A land with large, flourishing cities you did not build, houses filled with all kinds of good things you did not provide, wells you did not dig, and vineyards and olive groves you did not plant. These edicts are given with a strict precept: Be careful that you do not forget the LORD, who brought you out of Egypt, out of the land of slavery.

Anachronistically, we might notice deeply Burkean themes in this passage. The Israelites are commanded time and again to engage in acts of corporate remembrance out of gratitude for the unmerited inheritance the nation has received. This grateful remembrance is closely connected to the moral and political order of the nation:

In the future, when your son asks you, "What is the meaning of the stipulations, decrees and laws the LORD our God has commanded you?" tell him: "We were slaves of Pharaoh in Egypt, but the LORD brought us out of Egypt with a mighty hand. ...The Lord commanded us to obey all these decrees and to fear the LORD our God, so that we might always prosper and be kept alive.

It is on the basis of their shared history that the people are united and asked to bear fidelity to their God. He reveals himself as the God who delivered his people from Egypt and it is on the basis of this relationship, centred upon concrete historical acts, that the Israelite people are asked to trust God.[171] The Old Testament narrative shows a cyclical repetition of Israel becoming comfortable, prospering and deceiving themselves into believing that they are their own masters. Inevitably this precedes ruin, repentance and rediscovery of their identity.

For Christian societies, there is arguably an even stronger sense in which the moral community holds a narrative identity: 'The Word became flesh and made his dwelling among us. We have seen his glory, the glory of the One and Only, who came from the Father, full of grace and truth'. In this famous verse from St John's Gospel, Christians find ample reason to take history seriously. In Christ, God became flesh and amongst other things, affirmed the importance of historical narrative. Christianity cannot be reduced to abstract propositions in the manner of a philosophical system, as its logic is only comprehensible as the culmination of Israel's historical relationship with God and God's intervention in space and time. It is no coincidence that Judaism and Christianity have outlasted and outperformed all permutations of abstract philosophical systems. An emphasis on a moral community narrative can also be discerned in some other religions.

Within the community narrative the assorted symbolism of our daily lives finds its logical place. In his seminal anthropological work *The Interpretation of Cultures*, the influential American anthropologist Clifford Geertz dissected the importance of symbols. He argued that 'sacred symbols function to synthesize a people's ethos'. In particular, he noted the power of a shared religion to 'establish powerful, pervasive, and long lasting moods'. [172] In this, Geertz was an acolyte of Émile Durkheim, who spoke of religions as 'a unified system of beliefs and practices' which served to 'unite people as a moral community'.[173]

Such a clinically sociological approach need not necessitate a reductionism as to the veracity of religious claims, but they do help us to understand why religious belief is so essential to the functioning of a society and, in turn, why our moral values are so profoundly sensitive to us. A religious framework endows our transition through the various stages of life with meaning, from birth and adolescence, to marriage, childbearing and death: they are the intersection in our lives between the meaningful and the mundane. But is the idea of a shared moral tradition not impracticable and unrealistic in our modern world? [174]

Publicised comments from such figures as Lord Sacks, Rowan Williams and other spiritual leaders have tended to reinforce the view that a dominant Judaeo-Christian religious discourse in a nation, which provides the primary social and ethical understanding of the nation, serves to enhance the security of minority faith groups. The Conservative peer Lord Griffiths puts it this way: 'The claim, however, that Britain is a multi-religious society, far from undermining the need for a political philosophy to be grounded in religion, only strengthens it.'[175]

Christian Britain certainly has a far better track record of preserving religious freedom than many nations that have had secularism written into their constitution. Burke highlighted this fact when the atheist revolutionaries were attempting to extirpate religion in France. He believed a direct corollary of 'the destruction of the Christian religion' was 'a persecution which would strike at property, liberty and life'.[176] It was obvious to Burke that an established religion was the key to toleration of religion in society:

> I think that Church harmonises with our civil constitution, with the frame and fashion of our Society, and with the general Temper of the people. I think it is better calculated all circumstances considered, for keeping peace amongst the different sects, and of affording to them a reasonable protection, than any other System.[177]

In 1939, T. S. Eliot delivered a series of three lectures exploring these issues. The lectures were entitled 'The Idea of a Christian Society'. They offered a rich and robust defence of the belief that Britain, as a nation, was losing its common moral framework to the detriment of all its citizens. One of the things that troubled him about the trajectory of Britain was that it retained the vestiges of a Christian society, but increasingly its faith lay in democracy and liberalism, rather than any substantial system of faith.

Rather than starting with the fundamental questions of religion and morality and then working their way to politics, the new secularists held political forms to be fundamental and then aligned their moral beliefs accordingly. Eliot believed this faith in political forms would be worse for everyone in the long run. He was quick to point out that forms of government do not ensure any particular ethical content to a nation's character:

> It is only by returning to the eternal source of truth that we can hope for any social organisation which will not, to its ultimate destruction, ignore some essential aspect of reality. The term "democracy" as I have said again and again, does not contain enough positive content to stand alone against the forces that you dislike – it can easily be transformed by them. If you will not have God (and he is a jealous God) you should pay your respects to Hitler or Stalin.[178]

Such a warning portends the current crisis of confidence in an establishment which does not seem to offer anything more substantial than a vague faith in political forms.

Whilst Eliot wrote at a time in which Britain did not have the multiplicity of faiths that it does today, he thought that the moral leaders of the nation (or to use his term, the moral community) should 'include persons of exceptional ability who may be indifferent or disbelieving'. He also wrote that among the moral leaders there ought to 'be room for a proportion of other persons professing other faiths than Christianity.'[179]

In this regard, Eliot's vision is not dissimilar to the current constitutional arrangements in the House of Lords. The Lords Spiritual, that is, the Bishops, have held a place in parliament since the feudal period in which prelates would advise the monarch. Today, the House of Lords retains such a potential Christian voice in the form of twenty-six bishops, as well as a number of other Christian peers. Yet it is also joined by a host of experts in a variety of professional fields, as well as prominent figures from other faith communities.

Yet, as T. S. Eliot pointed out, a Christian society is not something that can, or should, be imposed from above, and the onus of choice must fall to the people of a nation. What is certain is that making no choice is not an option. If we do not actively choose a narrative and ethical vision then, as Eliot predicted, our society will fragment and reactionary political groups, the media, or the market will make the choice for us.

If we were to turn away from the ethically confused malaise of secular liberalism, what might such a society look like today? The most obvious point to make is that we cannot simply seek to turn the clock back. We have already seen that there were many injustices in Edwardian Britain which have rightly been remedied. Social, cultural and technological developments have also transformed Britain. In short, we should not be aspiring to recapture a bygone age, because no society, no matter how seriously it may have taken its religion, is synonymous with a religion. Rather, we should look to rekindle the traits which unified such a society.

This society would be one in which our understanding of humanity is governed by a shared narrative; it would be a society which publicly celebrates shared religious festivals and preserves a space for God in our public life; it would be a society which acknowledges the sovereignty of God in its highest traditions; it would be a society in which it is not considered unusual to overtly draw on religious ethical reasoning when forming public policy or arriving at legal judgments. There is no reason such a society cannot exist in our modern world. Indeed it does. Globally speaking, Britain's growing secularism runs against the grain. It is a choice that cannot be made at the political level but must be decided by ordinary people who shape a nation's culture. Whether the dominance of secular thought continues to prevail is perhaps the most significant ethical question of our time.

Chapter Eight

THE ENVIRONMENT

*The Earth will not continue to offer its harvest, except with faithful
stewardship. We cannot say we love the land and then take steps to
destroy it for use by future generations* – John Paul II

In 1974 the Australian minister for the environment, Moss Cass,
delivered a speech in Paris at a meeting of the OECD:

> We rich nations, for that is what we are, have an obligation not only
> to the poor nations, but to all the grandchildren of the world, rich
> and poor. We have not inherited this earth from our parents to do
> with it what we will. We have borrowed it from our children and
> we must be careful to use it in their interests as well as our own.
> Anyone who fails to recognise the basic validity of the proposition
> put in different ways by increasing numbers of writers… is either
> ignorant, a fool, or evil.[180]

Ironically, it was an Australian Labour minister, and not a
conservative, who made the logical connection between Burke's idea
of intergenerational obligation and the preservation of the environment.

In this chapter we will look at ecological conservation, as well as
the conservation of the human environment that we inhabit. The word
conservatism is the etymological cousin of conservation, yet they
are rarely linked in the public imagination. This is perhaps because
(predominantly US based) conservative groups have lobbied against
environmental conservation in the belief that it has been used as a vehicle
for governmental infringements of their civil liberties. In this conviction
they may to an extent be right, but the resulting antagonism has created
an overly simplistic dichotomy between care for the environment and

civil liberty. Going forward, it is a challenge for future generations of conservatives to place conservation at the forefront of their political agenda and re-establish the logical connection between the two ideas.

The natural world

Since the 1970s there has been an increasing global awareness that our world faces unprecedented ecological challenges. Climate change, plastics in the ocean, the deforestation of rainforests, the destruction of biodiversity and land contamination are all radical challenges in their own right, and together they present what seems an insurmountable challenge. To make matters worse, the destruction of the natural world is occurring at a vast rate. At the current rate of deforestation, the planet will lose between five and ten per cent of its forests every decade. Sixty per cent of the world's coral reefs will be destroyed in the next thirty years and ocean life is being destroyed by plastic pollution. The most conservative estimates of the size of the Great Pacific Garbage Patch are around the size of Texas. These facts should give us all cause for grave concern.

The free market, an idea that is rightly celebrated in conservatism, must know limits. As we have already seen, there is no need to be ideologues of the free market; liberty is in the main a good thing, but it must be bounded and guided. There is no inconsistency in holding the belief that free enterprise is a good thing while acknowledging that businesses often operate at the expense of the natural world. From fisheries overfishing coastal waters to logging businesses destroying unsustainable amounts of rainforest, such acts are euphemistically known as 'externalising costs'. Where local markets may react negatively towards immoral actors, the global market has not had such an effective feedback loop to those it is adversely affecting, and this makes it a less accountable, and perhaps a less moral, system.

A good example of this was VW's decision to save money by fitting eleven million of their cars with emission test-defeating devices, a scandal exposed in 2015. One might also think of Western consumers who are happy to pay a very low price for clothing products without considering where the product was manufactured and at what human or ecological cost. In 1939 T. S. Eliot observed:

We are being made aware that the organisation of society on the principle of private profit... is leading both to the deformation of humanity by unregulated industrialism, and to the exhaustion of natural resources, and that a good deal of our material progress is a progress for which succeeding generations may have to pay dearly.[181]

Eliot was correct to identify that the common good which, with Eliot, I take to be the virtue and wellbeing of humankind in community, has been repeatedly subjugated to financial and economic interests in our modern societies. Neo-liberalism (the marriage of extreme capitalism and the liberal demand for autonomy) undergirds the problem. The tacit assumption of such politics is that there is always a direct correlation between profit and human wellbeing. The problem with this equation is that the excessive individualism which neoliberalism produces does not lead to healthy human communities or environmental sustainability, but instead it leads to relentless and unsustainable consumption. To be clear, it is likely that it is market generated innovation and competition that will provide the solutions our planet needs to survive.[182] Nevertheless, the market must be given limits in those areas in which it corrodes the natural world. There are two ways in which this will be effectively achieved.

The first, and most potent, is by the demand of consumers. If consumers refuse to buy products which have a negative impact on the environment, the market will respond far more quickly than it will under government pressure or legislation. Global businesses have historically been less accountable than local ones, since their negative externalising of costs does not have an immediate impact upon the communities around them. In an age of social media and television this is changing. Documentaries which expose businesses' culpability for pollution or the violation of workers' rights could have a significant effect on profits. When governments seek to impose regulation, multinational businesses often have powerful lobbying interests to counter this. However, when consumers demand a change and are offered accurate information about business practice, it is harder for businesses not to comply. The key to this being successful is the conviction and determination of consumers and the dissemination of accurate information about the conduct of businesses.

The second way to give the market effective limits is by means of intelligent state intervention. Such intervention should help markets to act as the chief engine for environmental protection while incentivising research and product sales in eco-friendly technologies. This is a path that an increasing number of states have taken in recent years. Perhaps the most influential global driver of renewable technology has been Germany which has spent over two decades subsidising green energy innovations; 32% of German energy is now sourced from renewable sources.[183] This approach has not been without its challenges. Yet what began as niche Western innovations have now spread around the world, with even China and India becoming interested in green energy use and technology innovation.[184]

Between 2010 and 2015 the UK government invested £25 million in green technology innovations which, among other things, helped fund a biogas engine that runs on landfill waste and windows that act as solar panels.[185] The UK government has also committed £557 million for clean electricity auctions in line with its Clean Growth Strategy, as well as providing capital allowances for businesses which purchase energy saving technologies. Overall, the UK is now decarbonising faster than any other G20 nation.[186] We have seen that conservatism has always held a place for government as the orchestrator of a basic standard of justice. While it right to insist that environmental concern does not give a government *carte blanche* to confound the operation of businesses, it nevertheless does have a role in assuring the preservation of the natural world and channelling the power of the market.

Green energy is a flourishing market that is likely to grow rapidly in the years ahead. The rise in green energy technologies over the last decade has been significant. Wind and solar technologies have led the way with a 1226% growth since 1990, compared with a 71% growth in coal and a 29% growth in nuclear energy. The possibilities for manufacturing and exporting renewable technologies are also burgeoning. The number of electric vehicles being sold is now rising by around 50% year on year. China, in particular, is aware of this and has rapidly become the market leader in producing wind and solar technology, as well as electric cars.

Finally, a reliance on green energy has other positive ramifications, such as releasing Western governments from their reliance on oil producing nations such as Russia and Saudi Arabia. In 2018, 37% of EU gas was imported from Russia. Given the difficult relations between Russia and the West, their influence over European energy gives Russia a considerable amount of political leverage. It also enriches Russia. In 2018, 67% of Russian tax revenue came from energy exports. In an increasingly multipolar world, in which American hegemony is challenged, it would be prudent to ensure that the world's largest market is not in the hands of potential adversaries.

For those who worry that being pro-conservation equates to negative economic consequences, this does remain a legitimate source of concern, as Germany's rise in energy prices has demonstrated. However, despite high initial investment costs and issues of intermittency, green energy sources are naturally replenishing and are not exhaustible in the way that fossil fuels are – a prospect that holds obvious economic appeal. The transition to green energy needs to be managed carefully, avoiding quick-fix policies and letting the market take the lead where possible.

The excessive consumption of plastics is another issue that is gaining global recognition. As Theresa May pointed out in 2017, the amount of annual plastic consumption in the UK could fill a thousand Albert Halls. A number of relatively simple measures have already been taken in the UK, such as the 5p plastic carrier bag tax, which reduced the use of plastic bags by 90 per cent in two years, and the banning of plastic microbeads. Such measures are a good example of where it is appropriate for the government to direct businesses. Encouraging industries to be more responsible in their use of plastics will make a significant difference in preserving the quality of our environment, both locally and globally.

A central principle of conservatism is to implement change where it is necessary or desirable. Environmental conservation is both of these things. It is encouraging to see that there is recognition of this across the political spectrum. One of the dangers in a democracy is that short term issues which have an immediate impact on the electorate can crowd out more remote or intangible concerns. The danger is that complacency towards less obviously imminent issues will lead to inaction until it is too late to find a feasible solution. Conservatives should naturally have an intergenerational perspective which causes us to be diligent in our stewardship of the world we have been given. The models of incremental and organic growth of the structures of society, advocated by conservatives, hold a natural resonance with the idea of sustainable modes of living which preserve our natural world.

The built environment

One area in which young people in Britain are increasingly frustrated is that of housing. One in six people in the UK is overburdened by housing costs.[187] Unlike most areas of the market, housing is a finite commodity, particularly in a country as small as the United Kingdom. There is a fine balancing act to be performed between preserving greenbelt areas and providing affordable housing, which enables aspiring young families to have their own home.

Consecutive Conservative governments have held the belief that home ownership is essentially positive. As housing minister, Harold Macmillan oversaw the creation of 300,000 homes a year. More famously, Margaret Thatcher's 'right to buy' policy was introduced in the Housing Act of 1980. This legislation stemmed from the belief that people who buy a property, buy into their community. The property becomes their responsibility and they take pride in their small stake of the neighbourhood. Michael Heseltine, the Chancellor of the Exchequer at the time, spoke of a 'deeply ingrained desire for home ownership' in the United Kingdom, arguing that it fostered a 'desire to improve and modernise one's own home... and stimulates the attitudes of independence and self-reliance that are the bedrock of a free society'.

Empirically, there do seem to be tangible social benefits that emerge from home ownership. A recent NatCen study shows that home ownership is strongly correlated to a sense of community and community cohesion.[188] While there has been considerable debate about the success of the 'right to buy' policy, the principle of property ownership creating a social conscience remains a conviction of the Conservative party.

As house prices in Britain have increased, consecutive Conservative governments have continued to incentivise home ownership. In 2013 David Cameron and George Osborne introduced the Help to Buy scheme, acknowledging that the huge increase in house prices was blocking many first time buyers from purchasing a property. Yet, unfortunately, since the late 1990s, house prices in Britain have increased faster than average earnings, due to ever growing demand for a finite commodity. As a result, housing policy from successive administrations sometimes feels like a frantic scramble to bolt on as many properties as it can in time for the next election.

Whatever the policy of future administrations, it is important that they consider the big picture. If we follow the path of relentless expansion then, like the Easter islanders, we will be so engaged in our work that we will destroy our nation. Already, levels of traffic, population density and use of social services are becoming unsustainable and, for many, materially degrading the standard of life in Britain.[189] Any future approach to housing ought to be long term and should be taken from a perspective which places housing within the broader context of the multiple facets of life necessary to ensure human flourishing.

Summary
As a political philosophy, conservatism has a natural affinity with environmental conservation, both locally and globally. As we have seen, conservatism is concerned with the preservation of the good things that have been given to us; among these things is the natural world that sustains us and enables our political societies to exist. Conservative administrations must work hard to reclaim the mantle of environmental stewardship. Conservatism is not about allowing free enterprise to generate wealth at any cost; rather, it should be concerned with finding a sensible middle ground between sustainable growth and being ecologically minded. Such an approach may involve curtailing the excesses of our appetites and, by implication, countering the individualistic ideology of liberalism. This will perhaps be the most significant challenge of all, for our governments and our species.

Chapter Nine

BEAUTY

Beauty matters. It is not just a subjective thing but a universal
need of human beings – Sir Roger Scruton

Conservatism has a long and enduring connection with the arts. Before
Edmund Burke wrote his *Reflections,* he published *A Philosophical
Enquiry into the Origin of Our Ideas of the Sublime and the Beautiful*,
which significantly influenced the way Europeans conceived of beauty
and the sublime as psychological categories. Before Disraeli was
a statesman he was a novelist, Reagan had once been an actor, and
Churchill was an amateur artist.

But why should beauty be important to a political tradition such as
conservatism? The answer lies in the philosophical roots of the tradition.
Conservatism emerges from a much broader worldview, which has
historically been rooted in classical philosophy and Christian belief. In
classical philosophy, as well as Christian metaphysics, there is a very
real distinction between good and evil, truth and falsity, beauty and
ugliness. [190] It is true that beauty does not, by necessity, coincide with
goodness or truth, but, as Roger Scruton observed:

> It is an ancient view that truth, goodness, and beauty cannot, in the
> end, conflict. Maybe the degeneration of beauty into kitsch comes
> precisely from the postmodern loss of truthfulness, and with it the
> loss of moral direction.[191]

Western philosophy has traditionally held beauty to be a key value
alongside truth, justice and goodness. The belief that beauty is not simply
a matter of subjective opinion, but has an objective reality, goes back at
least as far as the pre-Socratic thinkers of ancient Greece. For instance,
classical architecture is premised on the Pythagorean assumption that

certain proportions are objectively more beautiful than others due to their mathematical ratios. For Plato, beautiful objects participate in a transcendental form of beauty. In this conviction Plato was followed by later neo-platonists such as Plotinus, who argued that the beauty of an object was proportionate to its imitation of an ideal form. Early Christian thinkers adopted such ideas. Saint Augustine held that Plato's transcendental forms were ideas in God's mind. It is of course also perfectly possible to affirm that there is a universally shared sensitivity to beauty that is grounded in our evolutionary psychology.

Whatever philosophical approach one takes to beauty, it is more easily recognised than it is described. This has made the philosophical field of aesthetics notoriously hazardous and more resilient to systematisation than other areas of philosophy. Indeed, it was hardly touched upon between the classical period and the eighteenth century when Immanuel Kant revived the subject. Like many phenomena that are important to the conservative, beauty is both self evident and conducive to human wellbeing, but sometimes it resists a clear systematic account of why this is the case. Like love, beauty is intangible and yet we have an innate sense of it; it has a magnetism that illuminates our lives, but it is hard to articulate why. It can startle us with its immediacy, or it can be the product of long reflection. Contrary to the prevailing tenets of post modernism, beauty is not entirely subjective. There is clearly a subjective dimension to beauty, but both common sense and empirical studies tell us that there is a broad consensus of what constitutes beauty.

If you were shown a picture of Salisbury Cathedral on the one hand, and Slough trading estate on the other, which view would you rather your bedroom window looked out on? Similarly, which piece of art would you rather in your garden: Michelangelo's *David* or Marcel Duchamp's *Fountain* (a signed urinal)?

While the full story of twentieth century art would require volumes to describe, we should note a few important movements which have taken us to where we are today. At the turn of the twentieth century, a movement called Expressionism emerged. This movement was less concerned with beauty than in effectively conveying subjectivity, in particular the discordant and godless experience of modernity. Towards the end of the first decade of the twentieth century, cubism sought to deconstruct the world as it is and reconstruct it in discordant shapes to afford the observer different temporal and spatial perspectives. Dadaism, which began in 1915, was the culmination of this turning away from a classical approach to art. It sought to deliberately revel in the shocking, the vulgar and the irrational. This paved the way for the surrealism of the 1920s, which was self-consciously engaged in the exploration and celebration of the counter intuitive and illogical.

Each of these movements, in their own way, turned their face away from the classical endeavour of affirming the world through the distillation of beauty. When examining the exhibits at the Tate Modern art museum in London, a common response is incredulity that such banal ideas are lauded as art. The reaction is understandable, since once art descends to pure self expression, then anything becomes art, no matter how talentless or meaningless, and the enterprise itself is debased. Modern art is the aesthetic expression of modern philosophy – there are no transcendent standards, merely subjective expressions of personal truths.

No one would attend a recital of a novice violinist who had not learnt to play their instrument, because the sounds would be discordant and there would be no pleasure or edification in the experience, and yet this is precisely what modern art has become. Art historians identify the cause of this shift in the decline of religious belief, the rise of psychoanalysis through figures such as Sigmund Freud (see Edward Munch's *The Scream*) and a post-war disillusionment with transcendence. Instead of capturing beauty and raising our thoughts to a higher plain, the purpose of art has become to reflect the arbitrariness and deformities of modern life. From concrete aberrations in our cities to modern art that exults the profane, a world of functionalism and ugliness had replaced a world which (however imperfectly) aspired to ideals and values.[192]

In 1961 Piero Manzoni defecated in a number of tin cans and labelled them 'Artist's Shit'. The Tate Modern has proudly exhibited this for the last two decades. Its website of states:

Manzoni's critical and metaphorical reification of the artist's body, its processes and products, pointed the way towards an understanding of the persona of the artist and the product of the artist's body as a consumable object. The *Merda d'artista*, the artist's shit, dried naturally and canned 'with no added preservatives', was the perfect metaphor for the bodied and disembodied nature of artistic labour.

If this sounds like pseudo-intellectualism posturing as profound art, that's because it is. By the late twentieth century much modern art had indeed become both talentless and meaningless, perpetuated by critics whose careers rested on buying into the same pseudo-philosophical observations; no one seemed brave enough to point out that the emperor had no clothes.

For conservative thinkers there is a human and cultural importance to beauty. Edmund Burke argued that if we want our country to be loved then it ought to be lovely. If we hope to inspire the lofty ideals of duty and patriotism that create social cohesion, we must create a country worthy of those ideals. Just as no one would follow an uninspiring and degenerate leader, so a country must inspire the confidence of its people. The medium of artistic beauty is one way of doing this. As Roger Scruton puts it, the aim of true art is to 'show the real in the light of the ideal and so transfigure it'.[193] Four hundred years after his death, the Dutch landscapes of Kerstiaen de Keuninck continue to distil the mood of craggy mountain passes and enchanting rustic landscapes. Similarly, the classical and biblical scenes portrayed by Peter Paul Rubens still entice the observer to make an imaginative leap into the heart of the drama.

Beauty is not just a handmaiden to hedonism. It transcends us, confronts us and unseats our egocentrism. In doing so it prompts us to think of the world beyond our own concerns. At its best, beauty is communicative of enduring truths and values, which can be transformative, manifesting social fruit in diverse ways. As Professor Nigel Biggar has written, 'If beauty is a prima facie sign of scientific truth for mathematical physicists, could it also be a sign of theological truth for ethicists?'[194] This certainly seems true of the narrative beauty in Dostoevsky's novels or the artistic beauty in Rembrandt's 'The Return of the Prodigal Son'.

Beyond the narrow enterprise of modern art, there are still abundant signs of creative beauty in the West, particularly in film, music and digital media. Pioneers of CGI (computer generated imagery) are crafting new worlds and captivating experiences which immerse our senses, allowing film makers to craft narratives with pedagogic power. The film industry holds an almost unprecedented ability to communicate powerful messages to every social stratum. Needless to say, many directors do indeed use the medium of film to enrich and edify our culture: *The Lord of the Rings* and *Les Misérables* are both powerful examples of films with rich narratives replete with moral themes.[195] There are directors who helpfully use their films to caution against tyranny and dystopian government, *Blade Runner* and *Minority Report* being two films in this genre. Then there are those who tell faithful narratives to honour those who came before us, inspiring the best impulses of duty and gratitude in us: *Saving Private Ryan* and *Dunkirk* both focus on the sacrifice of allied soldiers in WW2.

Like an ever flowing stream, art will undoubtedly move in unpredictable directions, but history would suggest that the future course of art will be channelled by new technologies. Whoever the next generation of artists are, they should not lose sight of the tremendous power they wield. It is easy for great influence to become divorced from moral responsibility, a fact most tragically witnessed to by the effects of genres such as 'gangster rap'. Freedom of artistic expression is not something that should be excessively constrained by legislation. Rather, we should acknowledge that art is symptomatic of our cultural values.

If, as a nation, we value social cohesion and desire the promotion of particular social virtues, then as consumers we need to start buying ethically. The fair trade movement and consumer pressure on clothing firms is transforming the practices of foreign industries abroad. It is time that consumers acknowledged the link between artistic industries and negative social repercussions in our public life. Nothing will extinguish such industries so quickly as if we refuse to be impressed by facile sensationalism and pity rather than purchase it.

Conservatism and Architecture

Sitting above the ancient city of Athens is the Acropolis, a fortress that dates back to at least the fifth century BC. The jewel of the Acropolis is the Parthenon, completed in 438 BC. The Parthenon was designed by Pericles and it has endured as a breathtaking example of the classical Hellenic architecture which Greeks introduced to the world. Its Doric colonnade is decorated with a pictorial frieze and triglyphs; behind the colonnade were housed a number of breathtakingly ornate sculptures. The Parthenon was constructed with an incredible consideration of proportion and ratio, in the hope of creating an aesthetically suitable structure for the worship of Athena. The enduring quality of this architecture is undeniable. Over the course of two millennia, humans from around the world have marvelled at its elegance and beauty, while its basic form has inspired countless neoclassical imitations.

We have seen that in the common law tradition, a belief in an objective order of justice does not preclude the possibility of creating laws which are relevant and appropriate for the people they are designed to govern. Similarly, in architecture, a belief in an objective standard of beauty does not preclude the possibility of beautiful art and architecture having distinctly localised forms. In 1955 the Jewish-German architect Nikolaus Pevsner, gave a Reith lecture at the BBC entitled 'The Englishness of English Art'. In this lecture, Pevsner draws attention to the continuity of character in English architecture from the medieval to the twentieth century. For Pevsner, there are national characteristics, from our climate to our topography, that influence English art and architecture. He acknowledges that national characteristics are nebulous and prone to change, yet there is a distinct sense in which England has appropriated to its own character distinct forms of architectural and artistic beauty.

English architecture of the Norman period was heavily influenced by Romanesque forms, evident in both ecclesiastical and civil structures of the period. Durham Cathedral is the most stunning surviving example of the era; its simple dog toothed arches and grand cylindrical piers support a great stretching arcade which draws the worshipper towards the altar. By the 12th century the Romanesque was already exhibiting features of the early English gothic that would flower in the thirteenth century. The lanceted windows and clustered piers characteristic of this period are still visible across the country, their vertical forms hewn into the parish church of Uffington, Oxfordshire and Salisbury Cathedral. Over the following three centuries this style would organically blossom. The decorated gothic period saw the tracery and interior decoration become increasingly floral and ornate, characterised by quatrefoils, trifoils and tight mullioning. The perpendicular gothic, as the name suggests, evolved as an architecture that was more focused on straight lines. The period was characterised by fan vaulting on the interior, while flying buttresses and ornate pinnacles adorned the exterior, creating a similitude between cathedrals and jagged mountains peaks.

By the Tudor period, architecture took a leap forward: low arches, hammer beam roofs, ornate chimneys and brick masonry gradually became typical in the Royal Palaces, academic institutions and stately homes of the era. By contrast, the vernacular architecture of the period utilised half timber with wattle and daub, and occasionally brick. This Tudor architecture can still be found across the country, with some particularly characteristic examples in Warwickshire. During the sixteenth and seventeenth centuries, there was a return to classical forms of architecture, such as those exhibited in the European Renaissance style, which eventually morphed into the English baroque.

During the eighteenth century, Georgian architecture exhibited simple, clean classical forms, but with its own English innovations. The beautiful Spa town of Bath is the best preserved example of this style of architecture. Concurrently, Palladianism advocated a return to basic classical structures. Finally, Victorian architecture saw the flowering of an eclectic number of movements, many of which produced iconic structures which survive today. Gothic revival architecture, driven by men such as John Ruskin, produced buildings such as Keble College in Oxford, while Tudor and medieval imitation architecture remain an exemplary vestige of this innovative era.

In surveying the broad brushstrokes of English architecture, we can see Pevsner's point. Firstly, England has a distinctive tradition of architecture which has been enriched by tributaries from other traditions, but it has made them its own. Secondly, every historical style has aimed to achieve an enduring and aesthetically pleasing monument; to the likes of Pugin, Nash, Brown and Barry this was morally obvious. Yet, in the early 1950s a new breed of architecture emerged. In 1953, the British architects Alison and Peter Smithson coined the term brutalism. Such modern architecture was not intended to innovate a beautiful new addition to our cityscapes; it was instead driven by a counter-cultural, socialist ideology.[196] It is perhaps telling that the pioneers of brutalism, the Smithsons, resided in a beautiful

Victorian property in Chelsea. Revolutionaries rarely end up on the front line of their own revolutions.

The remnants of brutalism now litter our nation, in the form of dilapidated old tower blocks, synonymous with crime and poverty. A mere half century after they were built they are widely despised by the public. The self defeating nature of socialism is as true in architecture as in economics. Rather than promoting equality, socialist architecture gave the rich a monopoly on beautiful properties leaving the poor in drab, soulless buildings. To see the spirit of socialism embodied you do not need to look any further than the cityscapes that it left its peoples. From Pyonyang to the suburbs of Tbilisi, the grim standardised skylines are predictably soulless. A visit to the *panelák* of the Czech Republic or the suburbs of Bucharest displays the grim dreariness of state enforced equality.

Just as post-modern philosophers have developed a pseudo language, which ostensibly raises their concerns to a higher plane than everyday people, so the pretence that ugliness is appealing may gratify a small number of architects, but it is a blight for the common man and woman, who in the main think their works an eyesore. In 2009 a YouGov survey showed that 77% of respondents preferred traditional architectural styles.[197] The decline in architectural beauty is particularly worrying when there is strong evidence to show that our urban landscape has a tangible effect on our wellbeing.[198] Is this surprising? Beauty is often a by-product of affection. That which we care about, we nurture and seek to beautify. But like most things to which we devote time and energy, the investment reaps dividends. As Winston Churchill put it, 'We shape our buildings; thereafter they shape us.'

There is an implicit elitism about the imposition of ugliness against the will of the general public. It rests upon the assumption that regular people do not really know what they ought to like – that shaping our human environment is not for those who will actually live in it; it is for those who have a higher education and know better. The end result is that we have substituted public beauty for kitsch and brazen novelty.

There is an alternative. The Dorset town of Poundbury is a good example of a modern town built in continuity with traditional architectural principles. Its construction began in 1993, with the backing of the Prince of Wales. Some architectural critics have referred to it as a feudal throwback and scoffed at its traditionalism. Needless to say, these views are not shared by the average inhabitant. Poundbury is thriving as a town. As the architect Quinlan Terry put it, 'The silent majority like this sort of building'.[199] As a nation we must demand greater accountability of architects and councils who transform our public spaces. In a digital age, there is no reason that new building designs should not be subject to selection by a vote from the communities that will live with them. The ambition of architects must come second to the sensibilities of communities.

Traditional architecture need not be expensive. Indeed the simplicity of style and materials in much vernacular English architecture means that it is not. Moreover, the number of insipid 1960s concrete blocks that are now being destroyed due to their ugliness, or the poverty of the building materials indicates that, in the long run, beauty and quality craftsmanship remain a worthwhile investment. There is ample proof of this. People come in their droves to visit Edinburgh and Bath, bringing business to the cities, but who goes to bask in the beauty of Slough or Milton Keynes? Beauty draws us to its object and that brings its own rewards, not least economic prosperity.

Tragically, the twentieth century produced the first generation to leave the nation with fewer beautiful buildings than it inherited. Edmund Burke's belief that society is a contract between those who are dead, those who are living and those who are yet to be born, should be reflected in the desire to create monuments that will outlast our short span on the earth. In architecture, the shift from community mindedness and public duty, to egocentrism and immediate gratification, has scarred our public landscape. The degeneration of architecture is symptomatic of a culture which has refocused our minds from the enduring to the immediate, from the moral to the self-serving, from the local to the placeless. If we are to follow Burke's commendation, to make our land lovely, so that it may be loved, then we should begin by treating the sickness and only then will the symptoms subside.

Conservatism and the Countryside

The British countryside holds an inherent appeal to the conservative insofar as its patchwork of fields, hedgerows and honey coloured houses are the product of a millennium of sculpting and incremental additions. The beauty of these aggregated features could never have been dreamt up by one individual or one generation. What began with the division of shires into hundreds in the tenth century continued into the growth of market towns, local guilds, ecclesiastical institutions, agricultural divisions and industrial innovations. Over the course of centuries each generation has left its own indelible mark upon the form of the countryside, and most have changed it for the better. Roger Scruton writes:

> There is no political cause more amenable to the conservative vision than that of the environment. For it touches on the three foundational ideas of our movement: trans-generational loyalty, the priority of the local and the search for home.[200]

The British countryside illustrates why conservatism is such an effective force. The great state-run agricultural societies of history, for all the blunt force of their factories and fervour, have never crafted something as complex, elegant and enduring as the British countryside. The brutal Soviet policy of collectivisation provides an apposite point of contrast.

Between 1928 and 1940, Joseph Stalin carved up the Russian country and imposed a state-run system of agriculture, worthy of his industrial ambitions. Tragically, the policy of collectivisation in Russia resulted in the deaths of around ten million peasants. Not only was collectivisation spectacularly wasteful of human life, but the people labouring under the onerous system were wretched and repressed. In 1957 Nikita Khrushchev stated his aim for the Soviet Union to surpass US agricultural output within 15 years. Not only did he fail in his aim, but his project demonstrated the failures of communist centralisation. By the 1980s Soviet agriculture was not even producing a quarter of that produced by US agriculture and was importing huge volumes of US grain.[201]

Similarly, Chairman Mao took the advice of Russian planners and embarked on a massive programme of industrialisation and agricultural planning. His stated aim was to surpass British agricultural output within 15 years. Between 1958 and 1962, the so-called 'Great Leap Forward' introduced mandatory collectivisation of farms and, despite vast investments in the system, it resulted in tens of millions of deaths from famine. The end result was that it forged a soulless landscape of clinical divisions which proved economically unsuccessful. Long after the communist regimes of Stalin and Mao had been consigned to history, many British farms remain in the same families that they have been in for generations. Unlikely as it would have sounded 70 years ago, British landowners, tending to their corner of the countryside and treating it with a love born of familiarity and self-interest, have not only outperformed and outlasted their socialist counterparts, but they have beautified their country in the process.

The medium of agriculture vividly conveys one of the great truths of conservatism: the love of individuals for their small plot on our planet is the simple difference which can make all the difference.

CONCLUSION

In this book we have journeyed through a number of areas in our shared public life. I have made the case that conservatism has much to say to our modern world, not just as a political philosophy, but as a moral philosophy. In Britain today people crave community, family and meaningful relationships. Conservatism offers the promise of a strong civil society, in which neighbourhoods and families meet people's deepest needs. It offers us a vision of society in which those who know us best are empowered to help us when we are at our lowest.

We have seen that conservatism also speaks to the material needs of the poorest. It offers the hope of higher standards in key areas like education and healthcare. It encourages us to unleash all the passion and creative potential of those who want to make a difference, but are held back by the bureaucracy of excessive regulation. It promotes a culture which says that there should be genuine equality of opportunity for all, no matter what family you are born into or where you are from. Where you start in life will not determine where you will finish.

I have argued that conservatism is not opposed to government; in fact it insists on it. But it must be a government which know its limits. We have seen that a healthy government promotes law and order, as well as some important social goods, such as a security net for the most vulnerable, a system of education, infrastructure and defence. But a conservative government is not jealous of the public sphere. It steps back and allows the army of everyday people which compose a nation to do their bit in making our society a better place. In doing so it allows them to develop their talents as individuals and forge friendships with those with whom they find a common cause.

Finally, we have touched on the conservative belief that both the built and natural environment really do matter. Each generation is a steward of good things for the next. We have seen how liberal individualism neglects to account for the way in which communities are extended through time, from our grandparents to our grandchildren and beyond.

In this book I have argued that, despite their differences, socialism and liberalism both fail to deliver a credible moral argument. Where liberalism began in the seventeenth century as a Christian plea for toleration, it has been transformed into a creed of its own. Our society is increasingly bearing witness to the fact that regarding personal autonomy as the highest good does not nurture a common vision, still less a moral one. As for socialism, it has refused to learn that indiscriminate attacks upon the wealthy does not constitute justice, nor does it benefit the disadvantaged; it is an expression of anger which benefits no one. I have suggested that the ideologies of liberalism and socialism increasingly pursue common ends, both striving to undermine social, moral and economic hierarchies. Liberation from authority is their final end.

If we look to history, the blind ambition to destroy hierarchies, irrespective of their moral character, has caused misery wherever it has prevailed. Moreover, it has almost always led to radicalism before collapsing into authoritarianism. For this reason, I have made the case that conservatism matters. It doesn't just matter in electoral terms; it matters in a much more significant sense. It matters because it is a political expression of a belief in moral order. As such, its principles can mean the difference between human happiness and human misery, for millions of people.

I started this book with the story of a society collapsing. The October revolution of 1917 brought about a chain of events which ended in tragedy. We will never know the true toll of human misery which was inflicted on the Russian people by a handful of revolutionaries whose ideology set the stage for the evils of communist Russia. But what the story does tell us above all else is that our beliefs matter. Vladimir Lenin, the leader of the revolution, claimed that 'there are no morals in politics; only expedience'.

By contrast, the conservative philosopher Russell Kirk once wrote that 'Political problems, at bottom, are religious and moral problems'. Conservatives have always insisted that morality matters because, when all is said and done, our political ideas wear a human face. They are the difference between a child receiving a good education or being stuck in poverty; and between a mother being saddled with debt or thriving in work. Conservatism has given thousands the opportunity to achieve a better life, irrespective of background. It gives the destitute a safety net when times are hard, but helps to create jobs for when they need to find work again. Above all, conservatism holds community at its heart, in the belief that human relationships can transform lives in a way that government programmes cannot.

It is my sincere hope that conservatives will be prompted to reflect on the human heart of their own tradition, ensuring that it never strays into exclusivity or avarice. But I also hope that sceptics will reconsider their opinion of a tradition which has brought opportunity to millions and in the past has set Britain on a brighter path.

BIBLIOGRAPHY

ADAM architecture, 'YouGov survey published this week suggests people prefer traditionally designed buildings', *ADAM architecture,* <https://www.adamarchitecture. com/images/PDFs/YouGov%20survey_Oct09_results&followup.pdf>

Adam, Frane, and Borut Roncevic, 'Social Capital: Recent Debates and Research Trends.' *Social Science Information* Vol. 42, issue 2 (2003) pp. 155-183.

Amato, Paul R., 'Reconciling Divergent Perspectives: Judith Wallerstein, Quantitative Family Research', *Family Relations* Vol. 52, (2003) pp. 332-339.

and Juliana M. Sobolewski, 'The Effects of Divorce and Marital Discord on Adult Children's Psychological Well-being', *American Sociological Review* Vol. 66 (2001) pp. 900-921.

Angrist, J. D., et al., 'Student Achievement in Massachusetts' Charter Schools', *Center for Education Policy Research, Harvard University,* (Jan., 2011).

Argyle, Michael, Peter Hills, 'Religious Experiences and Their Relations With Happiness and Personality', *The International Journal for the Psychology of Religion*, (2000) Vol. 10, Issue 3, pp. 157-172.

Arnold, Matthew, *Culture and Anarchy* [1869] (Oxford: Oxford University Press, 2009)

Baldwin, Stanley, 'Final broadcast to the nation' [1937], *British Library Online Gallery*, accessed 10 Jul 2018, <http://vll-minos.bl.uk/onlinegallery/onlineex/voiceshist/baldwin/index.html >

Balls, Ed, quoted in Mark Ferguson, 'The growth deniers - Ed Ball's full speech', *LabourList,* accessed 8 May 2018, <https://labourlist.org/2010/08/the-growth-deniers-ed-balls-full-speech/>

Berrington, Ann, 'The changing demography of lone parenthood in the UK' *Centre for Population Change*, accessed 16 Jun 2018, <https://eprints.soton.ac.uk/364230/1/2014_WP48_The_changing_demography_of_lone_parenthood_Berrington.pdf>

Brooks, Arthur C., *Who really cares: The surprising truth about compassionate conservatism* (New York, NY: Basic Books, 2006).

Bruce, Steve, *Secularization: In Defence of an Unfashionable Theory* (Oxford: Oxford University Press, 2013).

Burgess, Samuel, 'Edmund Burke, the Common Lawyers and the Natural Law', in *Studies in Burke and His Time,* Vol. 27 (2018).

Burke, Edmund, 'Letter from Burke to an unknown person Jan 20, 1791' in M. W. McConnell, 'Establishment and Toleration in Edmund Burke's "Constitution of Freedom"' *The Supreme Court Review* (1995), pp. 393-462.

'Letters on a Regicide Peace', *The Works of The Right Honourable Edmund Burke,* sixteen volumes (London: C. and J. Rivington, 1826-27) Vol. XIII.

Reflections on the Revolution in France [1790] (Oxford: Oxford University Press, 2009)

Cameron, David, 'Hugo Young Lecture' [10 Nov 2009], SayIt, accessed 06 Mar 19, <https://conservative-speeches.sayit.mysociety.org/speech/601246>

Cass, Moses, 'Speech on Environmental Policy at the Ministerial Meeting of the O.E.C.D Environmental Committee in Paris' [Nov 13, 1974], *Australian Government Digest*, Vol. 2, Number 4, (1 October 1974 - 31 December 1974).

Central Intelligence Agency, 'Country Comparison: GDP – Per Capita', *Central Intelligence Agency*, <https://www.cia.gov/library/publications/the-world-factbook/rankorder/2004rank.html>

Centre for Social Justice, 'The Future of Work: Regional Revolution', *Centre for Social Justice*, accessed 15 Sep 18 <https://www.centreforsocialjustice.org.uk/library/the-future-of-work-regional-revolution>

Chafuen, Alejandro A., *Faith and Liberty: The Economic Thought of the Late Scholastics* (Lanham, MD: Lexington Books, 2003).

Charities Aid Foundation, 'CAF World Giving Index 2018', CAF Online, accessed 07 Mar 19, <https://www.cafonline.org/docs/default-source/about-us-publications/caf_wgi2018_report_webnopw_2379a_261018.pdf>

Cherlin, Andrew J., P. Lindsay Chase-Lansdale, and Christine McRae, 'Effects of Parental Divorce on Mental Health throughout the Life Course,' *American Sociological Review* Vol. 63 (1998) pp. 239-249.

Christoffersen, Henrik, Martin Paldam, and Allan H. Würtz, 'Public versus Private Production and Economies of Scale', *Public Choice* 130, no. 3/4 (2007), pp. 311-28.

Civitas 'EHRC Refuses Britain a Fair Hearing', *Civitas*, accessed 12 Jul 2018 <http://www.civitas.org.uk/press/ehrc-refuses-britain-a-fair-hearing/>

Clark, Pitta, 'The Big Green Bang: how renewable energy became unstoppable', *The Financial Times*, accessed 12 May 2018 <https://www.ft.com/content/44ed7e90-3960-11e7-ac89-b01cc67cfeec>

CNN World News, 'Amid clashes, Greek Parliament approves austerity measures', *CNN News,* accessed 12 Mar 2018, <http://edition.cnn.com/2012/02/12/world/europe/greece-debt-crisis/index.html>

Cowley, Philip, Robert Ford and Isabel Hardman, *More sex, lies and the ballot box: another fifty things you need to know about elections* (London: Biteback Publishing, 2016).

Crehan, Lucy, *Clever Lands: The secrets behind the success of the world's education superpowers* (London: Unbound, 2016).

Danczuk, Simon, 'Cheap immigrant labour has cost blue-collar Britain dear', *The Telegraph*, accessed 10 Aug 2018 <http://www.telegraph.co.uk/news/uknews/immigration/11202976/Cheap-immigrant-labour-has-cost-blue-collar-Britain-dear.html>

Davison Hunter, James, *Culture Wars: The Struggle to Define America* (New York, NY: Basic Books, 1991).

Department for Business and Richard Harrington MP, 'Government confirms up to 557 million for new renewable energy projects', accessed 2 Aug 2018, <https://www.gov.uk/government/news/government-confirms-up-to-557-million-for-new-renewable-energy-projects>

Department for Education, 'Children looked after in England including adoption: 2017 to 2018', *GOV.UK* accessed 23 Jan 19, <https://www.gov.uk/government/statistics/children-looked-after-in-england-including-adoption-2017-to-2018>

Department for Work and Pensions and Kit Malthouse MP, GOV.UK, accessed 06 Mar 19, <https://www.gov.uk/government/news/one-million-people-lifted-out-of-absolute-poverty>

de Pauw, John W., 'The Private Sector in Soviet Agriculture', *Slavic Review*, Vol. 28, No. 1 (Mar., 1969) pp. 63-71.

Duncan Smith, Iain, quoted in Matthew Holehouse, 'Iain Duncan Smith: welfare reform is like struggle against slavery', *The Telegraph,* <https://www.telegraph.co.uk/news/politics/10591755/Iain-Duncan-Smith-welfare-reform-is-like-struggle-against-slavery.html>

Dustmann, Christian, Albrecht Glitz and Tommaso Frattinip, 'The Labour Market Impact of Immigration', *Oxford Review of Economic Policy*, Vol. 24, Number 3, (2008) pp. 477-494.

The Economist, 'Germany's reunification 25 years on: Comparing Eastern and Western Germany in graphics', *The Economist,* <https://www.economist.com/blogs/graphicdetail/2015/10/daily-chart-comparing-eastern-and-western-germany>

Ellman, Michael, 'Soviet Agricultural Policy', *Economical and Political Weekly* Vol. 23, No. 24 (Jun 1988) pp. 1208-1210.

Fagan, Patrick, 'The Real Root Causes of Violent Crime: The Breakdown of Marriage, Family, and Community', *Heritage*, accessed 9 Oct 2018, < http://www.heritage.org/crime-and-justice/report/the-real-root-causes-violent-crime-the-breakdown-marriage-family-and>

Ferguson, Niall, 'Civil and Uncivil Societies', *BBC*, accessed 11 Aug 2018, <https://www.bbc.co.uk/programmes/articles/1n02Kr5c1XCGkZbw8wvbv5s/niall-ferguson-civil-and-uncivil-societies>

The Ascent of Money: A Financial History of the World (London: Penguin, 2012).

Finnis, John, *Natural Law and Natural Rights* (Oxford: Oxford University Press, 1999).

Forscher, Patrick, Calvin K. Lai, Jordan R. Axt, Charles R. Ebersole, Michelle Herman, Patricia G. Devine, Brian A. Nosek , 'A Meta-Analysis of Change in Implicit Bias' (2016); Tom Bartlett, 'Can We Really Measure Implicit Bias? Maybe Not', *The Chronicle for Higher Education,* accessed 15 Aug 2018, <https://www.chronicle.com/article/Can-We-Really-Measure-Implicit/238807>

Eliot, T. S., 'The Idea of a Christian Society' [1939] in *Christianity and Culture* (London: Harcourt, 1976).

Fortescue, John, 'De Natura Legis Naturae' in *The Works of Sir John Fortescue Knight, Chief Justice of England and Lord Chancellor to King Henry VI* Vol. I. (London: Chiswick Press, 1869).

Francis, S.H. Jones, and C. Wilcox, 'Religiosity and happiness: During adolescence, young adulthood and later life' *Journal of Psychology and Christianity* (2000) Vol. 19. pp. 245-257. Michael Argyle, Peter Hills, 'Religious Experiences and Their Relations With Happiness and Personality', *The International Journal for the Psychology of Religion*, (2000) Vol. 10, Issue 3, pp. 157-172.

Gaita, Raimond, *A Common Humanity: Thinking about Love and Truth and Justice* (London: Routledge, 2000) p. 5, quoted in Nigel Biggar 'On Defining Political Authority as an Act of Judgement: A Discussion of Oliver O'Donovan's *The Ways of Judgement* (Part I)', *Political Theology,* Vol. 9, Issue 3, pp. 273-293. pp. 286-287.

Geertz, Clifford, *The Interpretation of Culture* (New York, NY: Basic Books, 1973).

Ghemawat, Pankaj, 'Globalization in the Age of Trump', *Harvard Business Review* (Jul-Aug 2017).

Ghemawat, Pankaj, quoted in Sarah Green Carmichael, 'Globalization: Myth and Reality', *Harvard Business Review*, accessed 11 Jul 2018, <https://hbr.org/ideacast/2017/02/globalization-myth-and-reality.html>

Goodhart, David, *The Road to Somewhere: The New Tribes Shaping British Politics* (London: Penguin, 2017).

Department for business, innovation and skills, et al., 'Government invests £25 million in game-changing green technologies', *GOV.UK,* accessed 2 Aug 2018, <https://www.gov.uk/government/news/government-invests-25-million-in-game-changing-green-technologies>

Gower Davies, John, *Small Corroding Words: the slighting of Great Britain by the EHRC* (London: Civitas, 2011).

Graham, Jesse, and Jonathan Haidt, 'Beyond Belief: Religions Bind Individuals Into Moral Communities', *Personality and Social Psychology Review* (2010) Vol. 14, pp. 140-150.

Grieve, Dominic, in *From Thatcher to Cameron: The Journey to Compassionate Conservatism,* Kay Carter (ed.) (London: Biteback, 2010).

Guéhenno, Jean-Marie, trans. Victoria Elliott, *The End of the Nation State* (Minneapolis, MN: University of Minnesota Press, 2000).

Hamilton, Alexander, 'The Federalist No. 51' in *The Federalist Papers* ed. Isaac Kramnick (London: Penguin, 1987).

Hannan, Daniel, *How We Invented Freedom and Why it Matters*, (London: Head of Zeus, 2013).

Hardy, Thomas, *Jude the Obscure* (Oxford, Oxford University Press, 2002).

Harrison, Lawrence, and Samuel Huntington, *Culture Matters: How Values Shape Human Progress* (New York, NY: Basic Books, 2000).

Herder, Johann Gottfried, *Treatise on the Origin of Language* [1772].

Hitchens, Peter, *The Rage Against God* (London: Continuum, 2010).

Hogg, Quintin, *The Case for Conservatism* (London: Penguin, 1947).

Hordern, Joshua, *Political Affections: Civic Participation and Moral Theology* (Oxford: OUP, 2013).

House of Lords, Select Committee on Economic Affairs, 1st Report of Session 2007-08, 'The Economic Impact of Immigration' Vol. I Report, <https://www.publications.parliament.uk/pa/ld200708/ldselect/ldeconaf/82/82.pdf> *UK Parliament Publications.*

IBM Smarter Workforce Institute and Workhuman Research Institute, 'The Employee Experience Index', *IBM*, accessed 10 Jun 2018 <https://www-01.ibm.com/common/ssi/cgi-bin/ssialias?htmlfid=LOW14335USEN>

Jo Cox Commission on loneliness, 'Combating loneliness one conversation at a time: a call to action', *Jo Cox Loneliness*, accessed 19 Jun 2018, <https://www.jocoxloneliness.org/pdf/a_call_to_action.pdf>

Keenan, S.J., James F., *Moral Wisdom: Lessons and Texts from the Catholic Tradition* (Oxford: Rowman & Littlefield, 2004) p. x.

Kinnock, Neil, 'Leaders Speech, Blackpool 1984', British Political Speech, accessed 12 Jun 2018, <http://www.britishpoliticalspeech.org/speech-archive.htm?speech=190>

Kirk, Russell, 'Conditions of Freedom', *Commonweal* (Jan 13., 1956) pp. 371-373.

Kitsantonis, Niki, and Rachel Donadio, 'Greek Parliament passes austerity plan after riots rage', *New York Times,* accessed 12 Mar 2018 <http://www.nytimes.com/2012/02/13/world/europe/greeks-pessimistic-in-anti-austerity-protests.html>

Kristof, Nicholas D., 'Welfare as Japan Knows It: A Family Affair' [Sept 10, 1996] *New York Times,* accessed 10 Feb 2019, <https://www.nytimes.com/1996/09/10/world/welfare-as-japan-knows-it-a-family-affair.html>

Kullinane, Carl, and Philip Kirby, 'Class Differences: Ethnicity and Advantage', *Sutton Trust* (Nov, 2016), accessed 08 Jul 2018, <https://www.suttontrust.com/research-paper/class-differences-ethnicity-and-disadvantage/>

Layard, Richard, *Happiness: Lessons from a new science* (London: Penguin, 2005).

Lyotard, Jean-Francois, *The Postmodern Condition: A Report on Knowledge*, trans. Geoff Bennington and Brian Massumi, (Manchester: Manchester University Press, 1984).

BIBLIOGRAPHY

MacIntyre, Alasdair, *After Virtue: A Study in Moral Theory* (Notre Dame, IN: University of Notre Dame Press, 3rd Edition, 2007).

Marjoribanks, David, and Anna Darnell Bradley, 'You're not alone: The quality of the UK's social relationships', *Relate* (2018).

Mason, Rowena, 'Iain Duncan Smith: hire unemployed Britons rather than foreigners', *The Guardian*, accessed 06 Nov 2018, <https://www.theguardian.com/politics/2014/mar/21/iain-duncan-smith-hire-unemployed-britons>

McDermott, Rose, James H. Fowler, Nicholas A. Christakis, 'Breaking Up Is Hard to Do, Unless Everyone Else Is Doing It Too: Social Network Effects on Divorce in a Longitudinal Sample', *Social Forces*, Vol. 92, Issue 2, (Dec., 2013), pp. 491–519.

Mishra, Pankaj, 'The Rise of China and the Fall of the "Free Trade" Myth', *The New York Times Magazine,* accessed 10 Sep 2018, <https://www.nytimes.com/2018/02/07/magazine/the-rise-of-china-and-the-fall-of-the-free-trade-myth.html>

Morgan, John, 'General election 2015: which way are your university's staff likely to vote', *Times Higher Education,* accessed 10 Sep 2018, <https://www.timeshighereducation.com/news/general-election-2015-which-way-are-your-universitys-staff-likely-to-vote/2020070.article#survey-answer>

'General Election 2017: 54% backing for Labour in THE poll', *Times Higher Education,* accessed 10 Sep 2018, <https://www.timeshighereducation.com/news/general-election-2017-54-per-cent-backing-for-labour-in-poll#survey-answer>

NatCen, 'British Social Attitudes: Record number of Brits with no religion', *NatCen,* accessed 11 Dec 2018, <http://www.natcen.ac.uk/news-media/press-releases/2017/september/british-social-attitudes-record-number-of-brits-with-no-religion/>

National Association of Local Councils, 'About Local Councils', *NALC,* accessed 10 Oct 2018, <http://www.nalc.gov.uk/about-local-councils>

Nietzsche, Friedrich, *The Gay Science* [1882], trans. Walter Kaufman (New York, NY: Random House, 1974).

Nussbaum, Martha C., ed., *Aristotle's De Motu Animalium* (Princeton University Press, 1978).

Office for National Statistics, 'Population of the United Kingdom by Country of Birth and Nationality', *Office for National Statistics*, accessed 11 Aug 2018, <https://www.ons.gov.uk/peoplepopulationandcommunity/populationandmigration/internationalmigration/datasets/populationoftheunitedkingdombycountryofbirthandnationality>

Office of the Parliamentary Counsel, 'When laws become too complex', *GOV.UK,* accessed 15 Jul 18, <https://www.gov.uk/government/publications/when-laws-become-too-complex/when-laws-become-too-complex>

O'Hagan, Ellie May, 'Is there a magic money tree? Yes children, there is. But that's the wrong question', *The Guardian*, accessed 12 Jul 2018, <https://www.theguardian.com/commentisfree/2017/jun/06/magic-money-tree-theresa-may-banks-nurses>

O'Neill, Brendan, 'Britain's real hate crime scandal', *The Spectator* (Aug 2016), accessed 20 Jan 2018, <https://www.spectator.co.uk/2016/08/the-real-hate-crime-scandal/>

Park, Alison, Caroline Bryson and John Curtis (eds.), *British Social Attitudes: the 31st Report* (London: NatCen Social Research, 2014).

Paul, Karsten, and Klaus Moser, 'Unemployment Impairs Mental Health: Meta Analyses', *Journal of Vocational Behaviour,* (June 2009) Vol. 74. pp. 264-282.

Lawrence, D. H., 'Letter to Ada Lawrence', [9 April 1911], *The Letters of D. H. Lawrence: Vol. 1: 1901-1913* ed. James T. Boulton (Cambridge: Cambridge University Press, 1979).

Linn, M W, R Sandifer and S Stein, 'Effects of employment on mental and physical health', *American Journal of Public Health* (May 1985) Vol. 75 pp. 502-506.

Lord Patten quoted in Javier Espinoza, 'Lord Patten: University quotas will hit standards', *The Telegraph*, accessed 21 Aug 2018, <https://www.telegraph.co.uk/education/2016/05/16/lord-patten-university-quotas-will-hit-standards/>

Luckmann, T., *The Invisible Religion: The Problem of Religion in Modern Society* (New York, NY: Macmillan, 1967).

New Schools Network, 'Free Schools: The Basics', *New Schools Network*, accessed 5 Feb 2019, <https://www.newschoolsnetwork.org/what-are-free-schools/free-schools-the-basics>

Nove, Alec, *The Soviet Economy: An Introduction* (London: Routledge, 2013).

Paton, Graeme, 'Britain among world's worst for traffic jams', *The Times,* accessed 8 Aug 2018, <https://www.thetimes.co.uk/article/britain-among-worlds-worst-for-traffic-jams-jx0hh7xk8>

Putnam, Robert D., *Bowling Alone: The Collapse and Revival of American Community* (London: Simon and Schuster, 2000).

Hogg, Quintin, *The Case for Conservatism* (London: Penguin, 1947).

Ridley, Matt, and Bobbi S. Low, 'Can Selfishness Save the Environment?', *The Atlantic Monthly* (Sep., 1993) pp.76-86.

Red Cross, 'Trapped in a bubble: An investigation into triggers for loneliness in the UK' (2016), *Red Cross*, accessed 12 Nov 2018, <http://www.redcross.org.uk/-/media/documents/about-us/research-publications/health-social-care-and-support/cop-isolation-loneliness-tech-appendix.pdf>

Roberts, Andrew, *Salisbury: Victorian Titan* (London: Phoenix, 2000).

Rose, Heather, 'The Effects of Affirmative Action Programs: Evidence from the University of California at San Diego', *Educational Evaluation and Policy Analysis* (Fall, 2005), Vol. 27, No. 3, pp. 263-289.

Russell, Bertrand, *The Impact of Science on Society* [1952] (Abingdon: Routledge, 1985)

Scruton, Roger, 'High Culture is Being Corrupted by a Culture of Fakes', *The Guardian,* accessed 10 Nov 18, <https://www.theguardian.com/commentisfree/2012/dec/19/high-culture-fake>

'Beauty and Desecration: We must rescue art from the modern intoxication with ugliness', *City Journal* (Spring 2009).

'Conservatism and the Environment', *Roger Scruton*, accessed 30 Jul 2018, <http://www.roger-scruton.com/articles/281-conservatism-and-the-environment>

'Tradition, Culture and Citizenship', *Law and Liberty*, accessed 15 Aug 2018, <http://www.libertylawsite.org/2017/12/18/tradition-culture-and-citizenship/>

'Why Beauty Matters', *BBC2*, accessed 29 Oct 2018, <https://www.bbc.co.uk/programmes/b00p6tsd >

Selbourne, David, *The Principle of Duty* (London: Faber & Faber, 2009).

Seresinhe, C. I., et al., 'Quantifying the Impact of Scenic Environments on Health' *Scientific Reports,* Vol. 5, Article number: 16899 (2015).

Sidebotham, Peter, et al., 'Pathways to harm, pathways to protection: a triennial analysis of serious case reviews 2011 to 2014', *GOV.UK*, accessed 20 Jul 2018, <https://assets.publishing.service.gov.uk/government/uploads/system/uploads/attachment_data/file/533826/Triennial_Analysis_of_SCRs_2011-2014_-_Pathways_to_harm_and_protection.pdf>

Simpson, Ludi, and Nissa Finey, 'Understanding Society: How Mobile Are Immigrants After Arriving in the UK?', *University of Essex Institute for Social and Economic Research* (2012).

Sircello, Guy, *New Theory of Beauty* (Princeton, NJ: Princeton University Press, 1975).

Smith, Adam, *The Theory of Moral Sentiments* (London: A. Millar, 1759).

The Wealth of Nations [1776] ed. Andrew Skinner (London: Penguin, 1999).

Smith, Helena, 'Athens descends into violence as 200,000 march against austerity', *The Guardian*, accessed 12 Mar 2018, <https://www.theguardian.com/world/2012/sep/26/greece-violence-general-strike-austerity>

Social Mobility Commission, 'The adult skills gap: is falling investment in UK adults stalling social mobility?', (Jan., 2019).

Stanlis, Peter, *Edmund Burke and the Natural Law* (Lafayette: Huntington House, 1986)

'Edmund Burke's Legal Erudition and Practical Politics: Ireland and the American Revolution', *The Political Science Reviewer*, Vol. 35, Number 1, (Fall, 2006).

Swales, Kirby, and Sarah Tipping, 'Fragmented Communities? The role of cohesion, community involvement and social mixing', *Natcen*, accessed 12 Nov 18, <http://natcen.ac.uk/media/1571059/Fragmented-Communities.pdf>

Thatcher, Margaret, 'Speech to Conservative Party Conference, 1984', Margaret Thatcher Foundation, accessed 15 Jun 2018, <https://www.margaretthatcher.org/document/105763>

The Spectator, 'Awful consequences of repealing the corn laws' [16 Dec, 1843], *The Spectator*, accessed 11 Jun 2018, <http://archive.spectator.co.uk/article/16th-december-1843/10/awful-consequences-of-repealing-the-corn-laws>

Thompson, Damian, '2067: the end of British Christianity' [Jun, 2015], *The Spectator*, accessed 11 Jun 2018 <https://www.spectator.co.uk/2015/06/2067-the-end-of-british-christianity/>

Tocqueville, Alexis de, *Democracy in America: and Two Essays on America* [1835] Trans. Henry Reeve (Pennsylvania: Penn State Electronic, 2002).

Turner, Victor, *The Ritual Process: Structure and Anti-Structure* [1969] (London: Aldine Transaction, 2008).

Turner, Camilla, 'Majority of young people do not feel proud to be English, survey finds', *The Telegraph*, accessed 21 Nov 2018, <https://www.telegraph.co.uk/education/2018/06/04/majority-young-people-do-not-feel-proud-english-survey-finds/>

Wainwright, Oliver, 'A royal revolution: is Prince Charles' model village having the last laugh?', *The Guardian*, accessed 29 Jun 2018, <www.theguardian.com/artanddesign/2016/oct/27/poundbury-prince-charles-village-dorset-disneyland-growing-community>

Wilson, A. N., *The Victorians* (London: Arrow Books, 2003).

World Bank, 'The World Bank in China: Overview', *World Bank*, accessed 11 Aug 2018, <https://www.worldbank.org/en/country/china/overview>

YouGov, 'How Britain voted at the 2017 general election', *Yougov*, accessed 15 Oct 2018, <https://yougov.co.uk/news/2017/06/13/how-britain-voted-2017-general-election/>

Yuval Harari, Noah, *Homo Deus: A Brief History of Tomorrow* (New York, NY: HarperCollins, 2017).

NOTES

Introduction
1 YouGov, 'How Britain voted at the 2017 general election', *Yougov*, accessed 15 Oct 2018, <https://yougov.co.uk/news/2017/06/13/how-britain-voted-2017-general-election/>

Chapter 1
2 Edmund Burke, *Reflections on the Revolution in France* [1790] (Oxford: Oxford University Press, 2009), p. 96.
3 Robert Peel was the Tory MP for Tamworth and father of the future Prime Minister of the same name.

Chapter 2
4 Daniel Hannan, *How We Invented Freedom and Why it Matters* (London: Head of Zeus, 2013), p. 66.
5 See Frane Adam and Borut Roncevic, 'Social Capital: Recent Debates and Research Trends', *Social Science Information* Vol. 42, issue 2 (2003), pp. 155-183.
6 While our natural affections do not give us a comprehensive education in virtue, Jean-Yves Lacoste's description of the affections as the 'half light of ethics' is a helpful one. For a good account of the affections as the disclosure of moral first facts, see Joshua Hordern, *Political Affections: Civic Participation and Moral Theology* (Oxford: OUP, 2013), pp. 71-81.
7 Bertrand Russell , *The Impact of Science on Society* [1952] (Abingdon: Routledge, 1985).
8 The term *communitas* was used by the anthropologist Victor Turner in *The Ritual Process: Structure and Anti-Structure* [1969] (London: Aldine Transaction, 2008) to describe a spontaneous feeling of group unity and togetherness.
9 The initial aim of the EEC in 1957 was to 'preserve peace and liberty', by means of economic integration. Yet, as political union has followed economic integration the EU has arguably made the possibility of conflict in Europe more likely than it would otherwise have been, by curtailing the sovereignty of nation states.
10 This is well illustrated by the low voter turnout at EU elections in comparison to national elections. In the UK, EU elections have consistently attracted around half the voter turnout of general elections.
11 David Goodhart, *The Road to Somewhere: The New Tribes Shaping British Politics* (London: Penguin, 2017), p. 44.
12 Edmund Burke, *Reflections on the Revolution in France*, p. 198.
13 A colloquial name for the European Commission, European Central Bank and International Monetary Fund.
14 CNN World News, 'Amid clashes, Greek Parliament approves austerity measures', *CNN News,* accessed 12 Mar 2018, <http://edition.cnn.com/2012/02/12/world/europe/greece-debt-crisis/index.html>;
Niki Kitsantonis and Rachel Donadio , 'Greek Parliament passes austerity plan after riots rage', *New York Times,* accessed 12 Mar 2018 <http://www.nytimes.com/2012/02/13/world/europe/greeks-pessimistic-in-anti-austerity-protests.html>; Helena Smith, 'Athens descends into violence as 200,000 march against austerity', *The Guardian*, accessed 12 Mar 2018, < https://www.theguardian.com/world/2012/sep/26/greece-violence-general-strike-austerity>
15 Tony Blair and Jack Straw called for further reform of the CAP in 2005, arousing the ire of Jacques Chirac.

16 Jean-Marie Guéhenno, trans. Victoria Elliott, *The End of the Nation State* (Minneapolis, MN: University of Minnesota Press, 2000), p. 51.

17 Alex Tomsky quoted in 'The Nation State: Is it Dead?', *BBC World Service*, accessed 14 Apr 2018, <http://www.bbc.co.uk/worldservice/theneweurope/wk18.htm>

18 Central Intelligence Agency, 'Country Comparison: GDP - Per Capita', *Central Intelligence Agency*, <https://www.cia.gov/library/publications/the-world-factbook/rankorder/2004rank.html>

19 Pankaj Ghemawat, 'Globalization in the Age of Trump', *Harvard Business Review* (Jul-Aug 2017).

20 Pankaj Ghemawat quoted in Sarah Green Carmichael, 'Globalization: Myth and Reality', *Harvard Business Review*, accessed 11 Jul 2018, <https://hbr.org/ideacast/2017/02/globalization-myth-and-reality.html>

Chapter 3

21 Peter Hitchens, *The Rage Against God* (London: Continuum, 2010) p.65.

22 Evidenced by the figures for civic participation in the 1950s-70s. See Robert D. Putnam, *Bowling Alone: The Collapse and Revival of American Community* (London: Simon and Schuster, 2000).

23 The Economist, 'Germany's reunification 25 years on: Comparing Eastern and Western Germany in graphics', *The Economist,* <https://www.economist.com/blogs/graphicdetail/2015/10/daily-chart-comparing-eastern-and-western-germany>

24 Adam Smith, *The Wealth of Nations* [1776] ed. Andrew Skinner (London: Penguin, 1999) p. 119.

25 Alejandro A. Chafuen, *Faith and Liberty: The Economic Thought of the Late Scholastics* (Lanham, MD: Lexington Books, 2003), p. 34.

26 Adam Smith, *The Theory of Moral Sentiments* (London: A. Millar, 1759), p. 1.

27 IBM Smarter Workforce Institute and Workhuman Research Institute, 'The Employee Experience Index', *IBM*, accessed 10 Jun 2018 <https://www-01.ibm.com/common/ssi/cgi-bin/ssialias?htmlfid=LOW14335USEN>

28 A study in the USA found that conservative minded people give substantially more money to charity and volunteer more charitable hours than their left wing contemporaries. Arthur C. Brooks, *Who really cares: The surprising truth about compassionate conservatism* (New York, NY: Basic Books, 2006).

29 Cigarettes, for example, are valued by many consumers in spite of their detrimental effects. This is why it is right that they are taxed by the government which has to fund the healthcare of smokers.

30 Alexis de Tocqueville, *Democracy in America,* trans. Henry Reeve (Pennsylvania: Penn State Electronic, 2002), p. 583.

31 Alexis de Tocqueville, *Democracy in America*, p. 583.

32 John W. de Pauw, 'The Private Sector in Soviet Agriculture', *Slavic Review*, Vol. 28, No. 1 (Mar., 1969), pp. 63-71, p. 63.

33 Henrik Christoffersen, Martin Paldam, and Allan H. Würtz, 'Public versus Private Production and Economies of Scale', *Public Choice* 130, no. 3/4 (2007), pp. 311-28.

34 Ellie May O'Hagan, 'Is there a magic money tree? Yes children, there is. But that's the wrong question', *The Guardian*, accessed 12 Jul 2018, <https://www.theguardian.com/commentisfree/2017/jun/06/magic-money-tree-theresa-may-banks-nurses>

35 Something also achieved by the multiplier effect of commercial bank loans.

36 George A. Akerlof and Robert J. Shiller, *Animal Spirits: How Human Psychology Drives the Economy, and Why it Matters for Global Capitalism* (Princeton, NJ: Princeton University Press, 2009).

37 The necessity for government goes hand in glove with the necessity for a healthy culture, which is not solely focused on the acquisition of material wealth as the end of society.

38 The Spectator, 'Awful consequences of repealing the corn laws' [16 December, 1843], *The Spectator*, accessed 11 Jun 2018, <http://archive.spectator.co.uk/article/16th-december-1843/10/awful-consequences-of-repealing-the-corn-laws>

39 A. N. Wilson, *The Victorians* (London: Arrow Books, 2003), p. 429.

40 A. N. Wilson, *The Victorians*, p. 428.

41 Neil Kinnock, 'Leaders Speech, Blackpool 1984', *British Political Speech*, accessed 12 Jun 2018, <http://www.britishpoliticalspeech.org/speech-archive.htm?speech=190>

42 A contemporary Gallup poll showed that 79% of people disapproved of the strikes.

43 Margaret Thatcher, 'Speech to Conservative Party Conference, 1984', *Margaret Thatcher Foundation*, accessed 15 Jun 2018, <https://www.margaretthatcher.org/document/105763>

44 Pankaj Mishra, 'The Rise of China and the Fall of the "Free Trade" Myth', *The New York Times Magazine,* accessed 10 Sep 2018, <https://www.nytimes.com/2018/02/07/magazine/the-rise-of-china-and-the-fall-of-the-free-trade-myth.html>

45 Alison Park, Caroline Bryson and John Curtis (eds.), *British Social Attitudes: the 31st Report* (London: Natcen Social Research, 2014).

46 Ludi Simpson and Nissa Finey, 'Understanding Society: How Mobile Are Immigrants After Arriving in the UK?', *University of Essex Institute for Social and Economic Research* (2012), quoted in David Goodhart, *The Road to Somewhere*, p. 4.

47 Margaret Thatcher, 'Speech to Conservative Party Conference' [1984], *Margaret Thatcher Foundation*, accessed 11 Aug 2018 <https://www.margaretthatcher.org/document/105763>

48 Alison Park, Caroline Bryson and John Curtis (eds.), *British Social Attitudes: the 31st Report*, p. 79.

49 Simon Danczuk, 'Cheap immigrant labour has cost blue-collar Britain dear' [2 Nov 2014], *The Telegraph*, accessed 10 Aug 2018 <http://www.telegraph.co.uk/news/uknews/immigration/11202976/Cheap-immigrant-labour-has-cost-blue-collar-Britain-dear.html>

50 M W Linn, R Sandifer and S Stein, 'Effects of employment on mental and physical health', *American Journal of Public Health* (May 1985) Vol. 75, pp. 502-506.

51 Karsten Paul and Klaus Moser, 'Unemployment Impairs Mental Health: Meta Analyses', *Journal of Vocational Behaviour,* (June 2009) Vol. 74, pp. 264-282.

52 David Goodhart, *The Road to Somewhere*, p. 52.

53 House of Lords, Select Committee on Economic Affairs, 1st Report of Session 2007-08, 'The Economic Impact of Immigration' Vol. I Report, <https://www.publications.parliament.uk/pa/ld200708/ldselect/ldeconaf/82/82.pdf>, *UK Parliament Publications*, p. 58.

54 House of Lords, Select Committee on Economic Affairs, 1st Report of Session 2007-08, 'The Economic Impact of Immigration' Vol. I Report, p. 59.

55 Christian Dustmann, Albrecht Glitz and Tommaso Frattinip, 'The Labour Market Impact of Immigration', *Oxford Review of Economic Policy*, Vol. 24, Number 3, (2008), pp. 477-494. p. 491.

56 Rowena Mason, 'Iain Duncan Smith: hire unemployed Britons rather than foreigners', *The Guardian*, accessed 06 Nov 2018, <https://www.theguardian.com/politics/2014/mar/21/iain-duncan-smith-hire-unemployed-britons>

57 Centre for Social Justice, 'The Future of Work: Regional Revolution', *Centre for Social Justice*, accessed 15 Sep 18 <https://www.centreforsocialjustice.org.uk/library/the-future-of-work-regional-revolution>

58 Lucy Crehan, *Clever Lands*, p. 264.

59 Lucy Crehan, *Clever Lands*, p. 265.

60 An expression used by Niall Ferguson in his Reith Lectures.

61 31% of Free Schools are outstanding compared to a national average of 21%. See New Schools Network, 'Free Schools: The Basics', *New Schools Network*, accessed 5 Feb 2019, <https://www.newschoolsnetwork.org/what-are-free-schools/free-schools-the-basics>; J. D. Angrist, et al., 'Student Achievement in Massachusetts' Charter Schools', *Center for Education Policy Research, Harvard University*, (Jan., 2011).

62 Niall Ferguson, 'Civil and Uncivil Societies', *BBC*, accessed 11 Aug 2018, <https://www.bbc.co.uk/programmes/articles/1n02Kr5c1XCGkZbw8wvbv5s/niall-ferguson-civil-and-uncivil-societies>

63 Social Mobility Commission, 'The adult skills gap: is falling investment in UK adults stalling social mobility?', (Jan., 2019).

64 Iain Duncan Smith quoted in Matthew Holehouse, 'Iain Duncan Smith: welfare reform is like struggle against slavery', *The Telegraph*, <https://www.telegraph.co.uk/news/politics/10591755/Iain-Duncan-Smith-welfare-reform-is-like-struggle-against-slavery.html>

Chapter 4

65 Peter Stanlis, 'Edmund Burke's Legal Erudition and Practical Politics: Ireland and the American Revolution', *The Political Science Reviewer*, Vol. 35, Number 1, (Fall, 2006) p. 67. Edmund Burke self-confessedly received his ideas of conservation from the common law tradition. Burke was deeply engaged with this tradition and repeatedly referenced its great figures in his speeches, even stating in parliament that he had been conversant with the common law throughout his life.

66 Samuel Burgess, 'Edmund Burke, the Common Lawyers and the Natural Law', in *Studies in Burke and His Time*, Vol. 27 (2018).

67 Clearly there are philosophical alternatives to this conclusion. The full case for a natural moral law has been made in substantial detail elsewhere. See John Finnis, *Natural Law and Natural Rights* (Oxford: Oxford University Press, 1999) For the purpose of this chapter the point need only be made that the natural law tradition has predominated in conservative thought, over alternative positions such as the rational calculus of utilitarianism or a reductionist evolutionary psychology.

68 For Fortescue 'all human laws are, as it were, instruments whereby the Divine law develops its virtues in human actions', helping humans to realise their created purpose. Fortescue, 'De Natura Legis Naturae' in *The Works of Sir John Fortescue Knight, Chief Justice of England and Lord Chancellor to King Henry VI* Vol. I. (London: Chiswick Press, 1869), p. 243.

69 This idea of human flourishing was taken into the Christian tradition by Saint Ambrose of Milan and subsequently expounded by Thomas Aquinas. For Aquinas, if we are to flourish as human beings, then in opposition to the claims of liberalism we should not

just pursue whatever we like, but we ought to pursue those things that are good for us. Aquinas was clear that the pursuit of these things that are good for us will not only cultivate virtue but foster the common good in our society.

70 Martha C. Nussbaum, ed., *Aristotle's De Motu Animalium* (Princeton University Press, 1978), p. 71. Some might question whether modern science provides an answer for this question in terms of DNA. It is true that DNA gives weight to the idea that simply looking like a lion does not make one a lion; there is a whole genetic code which creates something with the temperament and behaviours of a lion. But DNA alone does not render Aristotle's account redundant. Philosophers will be acquainted with Aristotle's distinction between the four types of causation: material, formal, efficient and final. The discovery of DNA would offer an account of the efficient causation of a zygote turning into a lion. It might even offer a formal cause for the design of a lion. But the question of final causation, the key idea in teleology, remains in the realm of metaphysics.

71 Russell Kirk, 'Conditions of Freedom', *Commonweal* (January 13, 1956) pp. 371-373.

72 Kirby Swales and Sarah Tipping, 'Fragmented Communities? The role of cohesion, community involvement and social mixing', *Natcen*, accessed 12 Nov 18, <http://natcen.ac.uk/media/1571059/Fragmented-Communities.pdf>

73 Department for Education, 'Children looked after in England including adoption: 2017 to 2018', *GOV.UK* accessed 23 Jan 19, <https://www.gov.uk/government/statistics/children-looked-after-in-england-including-adoption-2017-to-2018>

74 Peter Sidebotham et al., 'Pathways to harm, pathways to protection: a triennial analysis of serious case reviews 2011 to 2014', *GOV.UK*, accessed 20 Jul 2018, <https://assets.publishing.service.gov.uk/government/uploads/system/uploads/attachment_data/file/533826/Triennial_Analysis_of_SCRs_2011-2014_-_Pathways_to_harm_and_protection.pdf>, p. 75.

75 Ryan Messmore, 'A Moral Case Against Big Government: How Government Shapes the Character, Vision and Values of Citizens', *The Heritage Foundation*, accessed 21 Oct 2018, <https://www.heritage.org/political-process/report/moral-case-against-big-government-how-government-shapes-the-character#_ftnref17>

76 Oliver O'Donovan, *The Ways of Judgement* (Cambridge: Eerdmans, 2005) p. 61.

77 Alexander Hamilton, 'The Federalist No. 51' in *The Federalist Papers* ed. Isaac Kramnick (London: Penguin, 1987), p. 320.

78 Alexis de Tocqueville, *Democracy in America*, p. 584.

79 The Soviet Union was similarly intolerant of free association and trade unions.

80 David Cameron, 'Hugo Young Lecture' [10 Nov 2009], *SayIt*, accessed 06 Mar 19, <https://conservative-speeches.sayit.mysociety.org/speech/601246>

81 Department for Work and Pensions and Kit Malthouse MP, *GOV.UK*, accessed 06 Mar 19, <https://www.gov.uk/government/news/one-million-people-lifted-out-of-absolute-poverty>

82 Centre for Social Justice, 'Signed On, Written Off: An inquiry into welfare dependency in Britain' (May, 2013).

83 Most infamously EU Commision regulation No. 2257/94.

84 Alexis de Tocqueville, *Democracy in America*, pp. 770-771.

85 Office of the Parliamentary Counsel, 'When laws become too complex', *GOV.UK*, accessed 15 Jul 18, <https://www.gov.uk/government/publications/when-laws-become-too-complex/when-laws-become-too-complex>

86 John Morgan, 'General election 2015: which way are your university's staff

likely to vote', *Times Higher Education,* accessed 10 Sep 2018, < https://www.timeshighereducation.com/news/general-election-2015-which-way-are-your-universitys-staff-likely-to-vote/2020070.article#survey-answer>

87 John Morgan, 'General Election 2017: 54% backing for Labour in THE poll', *Times Higher Education,* accessed 10 Sep 2018, <https://www.timeshighereducation.com/news/general-election-2017-54-per-cent-backing-for-labour-in-poll#survey-answer>

88 Since 2008 a hate crime has been defined as 'any criminal offence which is perceived by the victim or any other person, to be motivated by hostility or prejudice, based on a person's disability or perceived disability; race or perceived race; or religion or perceived religion; or sexual orientation or perceived sexual orientation or transgender identity or perceived transgender identity'. This definition takes the judgement of what constitutes a hate crime away from any objective assessment and places it squarely with the subjective feelings of an individual, apparently obviating the need for impartial scrutiny towards the objective facts of a case.

89 Jo Johnson, 'Free speech in the liberal university' [26 Dec 2017], *GOV.UK*, accessed 14 Dec 2018, <https://www.gov.uk/government/speeches/free-speech-in-the-liberal-university>

90 Philip Cowley, Robert Ford and Isabel Hardman, *More sex, lies and the ballot box: another fifty things you need to know about elections* (London: Biteback Publishing, 2016).

91 An argument made by postmodern philosophers. See Jean-Francois Lyotard, *The Postmodern Condition: A Report on Knowledge* , trans. Geoff Bennington and Brian Massumi, (Manchester: Manchester University Press, 1984).

92 The myth emerges from the early modern period. The basic arguments come from a Christian narrative, but they lack a more comprehensive theological picture which gives context to their claims. Humans are equal, but only before God, humans do have an inherent dignity, but only as God's creation.

93 Raimond Gaita, *A Common Humanity: Thinking about Love and Truth and Justice* (London: Routledge, 2000) p. 5, quoted in Nigel Biggar 'On Defining Political Authority as an Act of Judgement: A Discussion of Oliver O'Donovan's *The Ways of Judgement* (Part I), *Political Theology,* Vol. 9, Issue 3, pp. 273-293. pp. 286-287.

94 Carl Kullinane and Philip Kirby, 'Class Differences: Ethnicity and Advantage', *Sutton Trust* (Nov., 2016), accessed 08 Jul 2018, <https://www.suttontrust.com/research-paper/class-differences-ethnicity-and-disadvantage/>

95 Social Mobility Commission, 'The adult skills gap: is falling investment in UK adults stalling social mobility?', (Jan., 2019), p. 8.

96 Patrick Forscher, Calvin K. Lai, Jordan R. Axt, Charles R. Ebersole, Michelle Herman, Patricia G. Devine, Brian A. Nosek , 'A Meta-Analysis of Change in Implicit Bias' (2016); Tom Bartlett, 'Can We Really Measure Implicit Bias? Maybe Not', *The Chronicle for Higher Education,* accessed 15 Aug 2018, <https://www.chronicle.com/article/Can-We-Really-Measure-Implicit/238807>

97 Heather Rose, 'The Effects of Affirmative Action Programs: Evidence from the University of California at San Diego', *Educational Evaluation and Policy Analysis* (Fall, 2005), Vol. 27, No. 3, pp. 263-289.

98 Lord Patten quoted in Javier Espinoza, 'Lord Patten: University quotas will hit standards', *The Telegraph*, accessed 21 Aug 2018, <https://www.telegraph.co.uk/education/2016/05/16/lord-patten-university-quotas-will-hit-standards/>

NOTES

99 John Gower Davies, *Small Corroding Words: the slighting of Great Britain by the EHRC* (London: Civitas, 2011).

100 Civitas 'EHRC Refuses Britain a Fair Hearing', *Civitas*, accessed 12 Jul 2018, <http://www.civitas.org.uk/press/ehrc-refuses-britain-a-fair-hearing/>

Chapter 5

101 Alexis de Tocqueville, *Democracy in America*, p.770.

102 David Selbourne, *The Principle of Duty* (London: Faber & Faber, 2009), p. 18.

103 David Cameron, 'Hugo Young Lecture' [10 Nov 2009].

104 Richard Layard, *Happiness: Lessons from a new science* (London: Penguin, 2005).

105 David Marjoribanks and Anna Darnell Bradley, 'You're not alone: The quality of the UK's social relationships', *Relate* (2018) pp. 14-15. Red Cross, 'Trapped in a bubble: An investigation into triggers for loneliness in the UK' (2016), accessed 12 Nov 2018, <http://www.redcross.org.uk/-/media/documents/about-us/research-publications/health-social-care-and-support/co-p-isolation-loneliness-tech-appendix.pdf>

106 Jo Cox Commission on loneliness, 'Combating loneliness one conversation at a time: a call to action', *Jo Cox Loneliness*, accessed 19 Jun 2018, <https://www.jocoxloneliness.org/pdf/a_call_to_action.pdf>, p. 7.

107 Kirby Swales and Sarah Tipping, 'Fragmented Communities? The role of cohesion, community involvement and social mixing'.

108 David Marjoribanks and Anna Darnell Bradley, 'You're not alone: The quality of the UK's social relationships', *Relate* (2018), pp. 14-15.

109 Arthur C. Brooks, *Who really cares: The surprising truth about compassionate conservatism*, pp. 54-55.

110 Arthur C. Brooks, *Who really cares: The surprising truth about compassionate conservatism*, pp. 54-55.

111 Arthur C. Brooks, *Who really cares: The surprising truth about compassionate conservatism*, p. 5.

112 Edmund Burke, 'Letters on a Regicide Peace', *The Works of The Right Honourable Edmund Burke,* sixteen volumes (London: C. and J. Rivington, 1826-27) Vol. XIII, p. 174.

113 Ann Berrington, 'The changing demography of lone parenthood in the UK' *Centre for Population Change*, accessed 16 Jun 2018, <https://eprints.soton.ac.uk/364230/1/2014_WP48_The_changing_demography_of_lone_parenthood_Berrington.pdf>, pp. 4-6.

114 Patrick Fagan, 'The Real Root Causes of Violent Crime: The Breakdown of Marriage, Family, and Community', *Heritage*, accessed 9 Oct 2018, < http://www.heritage.org/crime-and-justice/report/the-real-root-causes-violent-crime-the-breakdown-marriage-family-and>

115 Patrick Fagan, op cit.

116 David Goodhart, *The road to somewhere,* p. 200.

117 David Goodhart, *The road to somewhere,* p. 201.

118 David Goodhart, *The road to somewhere,* p. 200.

119 Paul R. Amato, 'Reconciling Divergent Perspectives: Judith Wallerstein, Quantitative Family Research', *Family Relations* Vol. 52, (2003) pp. 332-339. Paul R. Amato and Juliana M. Sobolewski, 'The Effects of Divorce and Marital Discord on Adult Children's Psychological Well-being', *American Sociological Review* Vol. 66 (2001) pp. 900-921.

120 Andrew J. Cherlin, P. Lindsday Chase-Lansdale, and Christine McRae, 'Effects of Parental Divorce on Mental Health throughout the Life Course,' *American Sociological Review* Vol. 63 (1998) pp. 239-249. Rose McDermott, James H. Fowler, Nicholas A. Christakis, 'Breaking Up Is Hard to Do, Unless Everyone Else Is Doing It Too: Social Network Effects on Divorce in a Longitudinal Sample', *Social Forces*, Vol. 92, Issue 2, (Dec., 2013), pp. 491–519.

121 C.S. Lewis wrote: 'For the church is not a human society of people united by their natural affinities but the Body of Christ, in which all members, however different, (and He rejoices in their differences and by no means wishes to iron them out) must share the common life, complementing and helping one another precisely by their differences.'

122 Galatians 3:28 (NIV) 'There is neither Jew nor Gentile, neither slave nor free, nor is there male and female, for you are all one in Christ Jesus'.

123 National Association of Local Councils, 'About Local Councils', *NALC*, accessed 10 Oct 2018, <http://www.nalc.gov.uk/about-local-councils>

124 Leslie Francis, S.H. Jones, and C. Wilcox, 'Religiosity and happiness: During adolescence, young adulthood and later life', *Journal of Psychology and Christianity* (2000) Vol. 19. pp. 245-257. Michael Argyle, Peter Hills, 'Religious Experiences and Their Relations With Happiness and Personality', *The International Journal for the Psychology of Religion*, (2000) Vol. 10, Issue 3, pp. 157-172.

125 Dominic Grieve in *From Thatcher to Cameron: The Journey to Compassionate Conservatism*, p. 145.

126 Dominic Grieve in *From Thatcher to Cameron: The Journey to Compassionate Conservatism*, p. 146.

127 Dominic Grieve in *From Thatcher to Cameron: The Journey to Compassionate Conservatism*, p. 146.

128 Dominic Grieve in *From Thatcher to Cameron: The Journey to Compassionate Conservatism*, p. 146.

129 Office for National Statistics, 'Population of the United Kingdom by Country of Birth and Nationality', *Office for National Statistics*, accessed 11 Aug 2018, <https://www.ons.gov.uk/peoplepopulationandcommunity/populationandmigration/internationalmigration/datasets/populationoftheunitedkingdombycountryofbirthandnationality>

130 Alasdair Macintyre, *After Virtue: A Study in Moral Theory* (Notre Dame, IN: University of Notre Dame Press, 3rd Edition, 2007) pp. xiv-xv. It should be noted that MacIntyre is very clear he himself does not support free market conservatism.

131 Lucy Crehan, *Clever Lands: The secrets behind the success of the world's education superpowers* (London: Unbound, 2016), p. 224.

132 Camilla Turner, 'Majority of young people do not feel proud to be English, survey finds', *The Telegraph*, accessed 21 Nov 2018, <https://www.telegraph.co.uk/education/2018/06/04/majority-young-people-do-not-feel-proud-english-survey-finds/>

133 Charities Aid Foundation, 'CAF World Giving Index 2018', *CAF Online*, accessed 07 Mar 19, https://www.cafonline.org/docs/default-source/about-us-publications/caf_wgi2018_report_webnopw_2379a_261018.pdf, p. 12.

Chapter 6

134 D. H. Lawrence, 'Letter to Ada Lawrence', [9 April 1911], *The Letters of D. H. Lawrence: Vol. 1: 1901-1913* ed. James T. Boulton (Cambridge: Cambridge University Press, 1979), p. 256

135 James F. Keenan, S.J., *Moral Wisdom: Lessons and Texts from the Catholic Tradition* (Oxford: Rowman & Littlefield, 2004), p. x.

136 Roger Scruton, 'Tradition, Culture and Citizenship', *Law and Liberty*, accessed 15 Aug 2018, <http://www.libertylawsite.org/2017/12/18/tradition-culture-and-citizenship/>

137 Roger Scruton, 'Tradition, Culture and Citizenship'.

138 Thomas Hardy, *Jude the Obscure* (Oxford, Oxford University Press, 2002) p. 111.

139 James F. Keenan, S.J., *Moral Wisdom: Lessons and Texts from the Catholic Tradition*, p. 10.

140 Edmund Burke, *Reflections on the Revolution in France*, p. 33.

141 Oliver O'Donovan, *The Ways of Judgement*, p. 70.

142 It should be acknowledged that nations and cultures rarely share an identical locus. Culture is a more complex phenomenon than this. There are, for example, innumerable European philosophers, musicians and artists whose influence has bled into British culture. Equally, there are micro cultures within a nation state; Cambridgeshire has different traditions to Yorkshire. Yet, for all the tributaries of culture, there is a broad confluence which defines a nation.

143 See Oliver O'Donovan, *The Ways of Judgement*, Ch. 5.

144 Liberalism posits this moment of critical reflection and self determination at the very point of creation. The liberal narrative tells us that we are able to ethically determine our own ends before we have been edified in anything. This is the ideology of autonomy.

145 Burke, 'Reflections on the Revolution in France', p. 33.

146 Johann Gottfried Herder, *Treatise on the Origin of Language* [1772].

147 Clifford Geertz, *The Interpretation of Culture* (New York, NY: Basic Books, 1973), p. 89.

148 Lawrence Harrison and Samuel Huntington, *Culture Matters: How Values Shape Human Progress* (New York, NY: Basic Books, 2000), p. xxv.

149 See Niall Ferguson, *The Ascent of Money: A Financial History of the World* (London: Penguin, 2012), pp. 210-211.

150 Nicholas D. Kristof, 'Welfare as Japan Knows It: A Family Affair' [Sep 10, 1996] *New York Times,* accessed 10 Feb 2019, <https://www.nytimes.com/1996/09/10/world/welfare-as-japan-knows-it-a-family-affair.html>

151 Roger Scruton, 'High Culture is Being Corrupted by a Culture of Fakes', *The Guardian,* accessed 10 Nov 18, <https://www.theguardian.com/commentisfree/2012/dec/19/high-culture-fake>

152 Matthew Arnold, *Culture and Anarchy* [1869] (Oxford: Oxford University Press, 2009).

153 A point forcefully made in Karl Barth's criticism of the German churches of the 1930s.

154 T. S. Eliot, 'The idea of a Christian Society', p. 76.

155 James Davison Hunter, *Culture Wars: The Struggle to Define America* (New York, NY: Basic Books, 1991).

156 Brendan O'Neill, 'Britain's real hate crime scandal', *The Spectator* (Aug 2016),

accessed 20 Jan 2018, <https://www.spectator.co.uk/2016/08/the-real-hate-crime-scandal/>

157 Since the Edict of Milan in 313 AD, Christendom held a distinction between the functional governance of spiritual affairs and the temporal governance of the State. In Medieval Europe the Church retained spiritual authority, while rulers presided over secular affairs; this division of authorities gave rise to a number of tense face offs between monarchs and the Holy See. By the early modern period (in particular the Peace of Westphalia in 1648) there was increasingly a move towards spiritual and political authority being united under one ruler and a functional division between religious belief and temporal administration; a process prompted in large part by the reformation. Yet, properly understood the early modern separation of church and state was always a matter of institutional function, not conceptual separation. Even the most ardent advocates of religious liberty did not expect religious belief to be delineated from political theory; this was a later idea which was advocated in the advocacy of pure reason by the French *philosophes*.

158 Ronald Reagan, 'President's Speech to National Association of Evangelicals' [March 9, 1983].

159 Burke reminded the British people that 'we have not relegated religion (like something we were ashamed to show) to obscure municipalities or rustic villages. No! we will have her to exalt her mitred front in courts and parliaments. We will have her mixed throughout the whole mass of life and blended with all the classes of society.'

160 Lord Salisbury quoted in Andrew Roberts, *Salisbury: Victorian Titan* (London: Phoenix, 2000), p. 286.

161 Peter Stanlis, *Edmund Burke and the Natural Law* (Lafayette: Huntington House, 1986); Quintin Hogg, *The Case for Conservatism* (London: Penguin, 1947).

162 Friedrich Nietzsche, *The Gay Science* [1882], trans. Walter Kaufman (New York, NY: Random House, 1974).

163 Steve Bruce, *Secularization: In Defence of an Unfashionable Theory* (Oxford: Oxford University Press, 2013).

164 T. Luckmann, *The Invisible Religion: The Problem of Religion in Modern Society* (New York, NY: Macmillan, 1967).

165 Alasdair MacIntrye, *After Virtue: A Study in Moral Theory*.

166 Former Archbishop of Canterbury Lord Carey and former Chief Rabbi Lord Sacks have both raised concerns about religious liberty with the rise of liberal equality laws. Tim Ross, 'Chief Rabbi: Equality laws leading to new Mayflower exodus', *The Telegraph,* accessed 24 Oct 2018, <https://www.telegraph.co.uk/news/religion/8609531/Chief-Rabbi-Equality-laws-leading-to-new-Mayflower-exodus.html>

167 Noah Yuval Harari, *Homo Deus: A Brief History of Tomorrow* (New York, NY: HarperCollins, 2017), p. 355.

168 NatCen, 'British Social Attitudes: Record number of Brits with no religion', *NatCen,* accessed 11 Dec 2018, <http://www.natcen.ac.uk/news-media/press-releases/2017/september/british-social-attitudes-record-number-of-brits-with-no-religion/>

169 Damian Thompson, '2067: the end of British Christianity' [June, 2015], *The Spectator,* accessed 11 Jun 2018 <https://www.spectator.co.uk/2015/06/2067-the-end-of-british-christianity/>

170 Jesse Graham and Jonathan Haidt, 'Beyond Belief: Religions Bind Individuals Into Moral Communities', *Personality and Social Psychology Review* (2010) Vol. 14, pp. 140-150.

171 This is a pattern mirrored throughout the Old Testament, notably in the Ten Commandments 'I am the LORD your God, who brought you out of Egypt, out of the land of slavery. You shall have no other gods before me.' Exodus 20: 1-2 (NIV).

172 Clifford Geertz, *The Interpretation of Cultures*, p. 90.

173 Émile Durkheim, *The Elementary Forms of Religious Life,* trans. Carol Cosman (Oxford: Oxford University Press, 2008), p. 46.

174 Émile Durkheim expressed this idea with his concept of *anomie.*

175 Brian Griffiths, *From Thatcher to Cameron: The Journey to Compassionate Conservatism*, p. 71.

176 Edmund Burke, *Reflections on the Revolution in France*, p. 112.

177 Edmund Burke, 'Letter from Burke to an unknown person Jan 20, 1791' in M. W. McConnell, 'Establishment and Toleration in Edmund Burke's "Constitution of Freedom"' *The Supreme Court Review* (1995), pp. 393–462. p. 399.

178 T. S. Eliot, 'The Idea of a Christian Society' [1939] in *Christianity and Culture* (London: Harcourt, 1976), p. 50.

179 T. S. Eliot, 'The idea of a Christian Society', p. 29.

Chapter 7

180 Moses Cass, 'Speech on Environmental Policy at the Ministerial Meeting of the O.E.C.D Environmental Committee in Paris' [Nov 13, 1974], *Australian Government Digest*, Vol. 2, Number 4, (1 Oct 1974 – 31 Dec 1974), p. 1145.

181 T. S. Eliot, 'The Idea of a Christian Society', p. 49. Eliot goes on to write 'a wrong attitude towards nature implies, somewhere, a wrong attitude towards God and that the consequence is an inevitable doom.'

182 Matt Ridley and Bobbi S. Low, 'Can Selfishness Save the Environment?', *The Atlantic Monthly* (Sep, 1993), pp.76-86.

183 Pitta Clark, 'The Big Green Bang: how renewable energy became unstoppable', *The Financial Times*, accessed 12 May 2018 <https://www.ft.com/content/44ed7e90-3960-11e7-ac89-b01cc67cfeec>

184 Though in 2018 China still had higher levels of carbon emissions than the EU and the USA combined.

185 Department for business, innovation and skills, et al., 'Government invests £25 million in game-changing green technologies', *GOV.UK,* accessed 2 Aug 2018, <https://www.gov.uk/government/news/government-invests-25-million-in-game-changing-green-technologies>

186 Department for business and Richard Harrington MP, 'Government confirms up to 557 million for new renewable energy projects', accessed 2 Aug 2018, <https://www.gov.uk/government/news/government-confirms-up-to-557-million-for-new-renewable-energy-projects>

187 Shelter, 'UK third least affordable in Europe for housing costs', *Shelter Media Centre*, accessed 5 Jan 2019, <http://media.shelter.org.uk/home/press_releases/uk_third_least_affordable_in_europe_for_housing_costs>

188 Kirby Swales and Sarah Tipping, 'Fragmented Communities? The role of cohesion, community involvement and social mixing', p. 14.

189 Graeme Paton, 'Britain among world's worst for traffic jams', *The Times,* accessed 8 Aug 2018, <https://www.thetimes.co.uk/article/britain-among-worlds-worst-for-traffic-jams-jx0hh7xk8>

190 'Classical philosophy' is a term with limited descriptive value, but I am here thinking of Platonism, elements of Aristotelianism, as well as Stoicism. These are the three greatest influences on Western Philosophy in general, as well as on the conservative tradition in particular.

Chapter 8

191 Roger Scruton, 'Beauty and Desecration: We must rescue art from the modern intoxication with ugliness', *City Journal* (Spring 2009).

192 Some modern philosophers have pushed back against the subjective turn in modern aesthetics. Guy Sircello argues that beauty is an objective property that some objects contain in greater degree than others. He also draws a link between beauty and morality, speaking of moral beauty. Guy Sircello, *New Theory of Beauty* (Princeton, NJ: Princeton University Press, 1975).

193 Roger Scruton, 'Why Beauty Matters', *BBC2*, accessed 29 Oct 2018, <https://www.bbc.co.uk/programmes/b00p6tsd >

194 Nigel Biggar, 'On Defining Political Authority as an Act of Judgement: A Discussion of Oliver O'Donovan's *The Ways of Judgement* (Part I)', p. 275.

195 It is striking that two of the most morally edifying films in recent decades have been adaptations of books written before 1950.

196 Rayner Banham, *The New Brutalism – Ethic or Aesthetic?* (New York, NY: Reinhold Publishing Corporation, 1966).

197 ADAM architecture, 'YouGov survey published this week suggests people prefer traditionally designed buildings', *ADAM architecture,* <https://www.adamarchitecture.com/images/PDFs/YouGov%20survey_Oct09_results&followup.pdf>

198 C. I. Seresinhe et al., 'Quantifying the Impact of Scenic Environments on Health' *Scientific Reports,* Vol. 5, Article number: 16899 (2015)

199 Oliver Wainwright, 'A royal revolution: is Prince Charles' model village having the last laugh?', *The Guardian,* accessed 29 Jun 2018, <www.theguardian.com/artanddesign/2016/oct/27/poundbury-prince-charles-village-dorset-disneyland-growing-community>

200 Roger Scruton, 'Conservatism and the Environment', *Roger Scruton,* accessed 30 Jul 2018, <http://www.roger-scruton.com/articles/281-conservatism-and-the-environment>

201 Michael Ellman, 'Soviet Agricultural Policy', *Economical and Political Weekly* Vol. 23, No. 24 (Jun 1988), pp. 1208-1210, p. 1208.

INDEX